Ella

Who you are matters
and makes a difference!

P. Cen.

Breaking the Armour

PAIGE ORION

BALBOA.
PRESS

A DIVISION OF HAY HOUSE

Balboa Press books may be ordered through booksellers or by contacting:

Balboa Press
A Division of Hay House
1663 Liberty Drive
Bloomington, IN 47403
www.balboapress.com
1 (877) 407-4847

Because of the dynamic nature of the Internet, any web addresses or
links contained in this book may have changed since publication and
may no longer be valid. The views expressed in this work are solely those
of the author and do not necessarily reflect the views of the publisher,
and the publisher hereby disclaims any responsibility for them.

The author of this book does not dispense medical advice or prescribe the use
of any technique as a form of treatment for physical, emotional, or medical
problems without the advice of a physician, either directly or indirectly. The
intent of the author is only to offer information of a general nature to help
you in your quest for emotional and spiritual well-being. In the event you use
any of the information in this book for yourself, which is your constitutional
right, the author and the publisher assume no responsibility for your actions.

Any people depicted in stock imagery provided by Thinkstock are models,
and such images are being used for illustrative purposes only.
Certain stock imagery © Thinkstock.

Print information available on the last page.

ISBN: 978-1-5043-4272-8 (sc)
ISBN: 978-1-5043-4273-5 (hc)
ISBN: 978-1-5043-4271-1 (e)

Library of Congress Control Number: 2015954164

Balboa Press rev. date: 2/12/2016

Contents

The enclosed poem ~ "I close my eyes and take a breath" and "The Reflection" as well as the quotes that you read throughout this book were written by the author, Paige Orion.

Acknowledgments

To my Amazing Sons ~ I love you both with all of my heart. The two of you have taught me so much about life and myself. You both inspire me and make me so proud of the young men that you are. I am so thankful you chose me, in this lifetime, to be your Mom.

To Susan ~I know that you have found the peace and contentment that your soul so longed for. You have helped me to find my own strength which has encouraged me to tell my story in hopes that it will help someone to heal and find their own inner strength.

To my Family ~ I love you all and am thankful for your love and support throughout my life.

To my Mom ~ Thank–you, for the gift of your painting for this book's cover. It means so much to me. You created it from your heart, and it captures exactly the vision that I received.

Welcome

My journey to healing started many years ago, little did I know that along the way I would be guided and given tools not only for myself but for other people as well. I learned how to heal, embrace my spiritual gifts, listen to my soul and most important I learned to love myself.

I knew at a young age that I was different than my peers in that I could sense people on a soul level. I could see and sense energy, feel many things that they too were feeling, and that certain things such as people, animals, and events would show up, each one at the perfect time to guide me on this path of life. It took me many years to figure this all out, and I am sure there is much more to it that I have yet to experience but for now I am in awe and gratitude for exactly where I am at the moment for it is a place of peace and contentment.

This book is about my own healing, but is intended to help teach how we create each and every event that happens to us. I was guided through the whole process by my Higher Self and Spirit. The words flowed so easily and took only Eight days to write, and I am honored to be able to share it with you. I hope that you can take something away from it that may help you along.

The beginning of this book was hard for me to write, as it comes from a place of feeling like a victim, and yet that is exactly what I was at the time of the actual events at those times in my life, so I have to tell it from where I was at and not from where I am now.

I can honestly say that I am no longer a victim; in fact, I sometimes forget that these events even happen to me as I have healed them so immensely. I know that if I have healed them at such a great depth, then you can as well, it really can be done.

I was reflecting on how this book reminds me of my pregnancy with my oldest son. I was seventeen and scared. Scared of what people would think of me. I had a few people who wanted me to terminate my pregnancy, but I knew that this baby was to be born, and he has turned out to be one of the greatest blessings in my life. Like my pregnancy, I have had a few people wanting me to terminate this book, but, I know it is to be birthed.

I remember, going back to school that fall, seventeen and 5 months pregnant. Everyone knew of my pregnancy. My boyfriend had broken up with me and I really didn't have any friends. I remember telling my Mom how scared I was to have everyone stare at me and see me this way. She said "Paige, you go to that school, open that door and you walk through with your head held high and be proud of who you are!"

So here I am, holding my head high and walking through this door of sharing my book of life experiences with you.

Life really is an amazing journey. I believe full heartedly, that we truly do create our lives. We are more powerful than we can imagine and that life is a beautiful puzzle. Some parts are easy to figure out and others are more challenging but once we are done and take a step back we can see just how each event, each person and experience has been perfectly placed to fit with another piece. Each one connected to the next and it is us who are placing each and every piece along the way.

Be gentle with yourself; know that you matter, each and every person on this beautiful earth matters... Who you are makes a difference... The world needs you to shine like the magnificent light that you are.

Paige Orion

Chapter 1
Building the Armour

Ugly, stupid, scrawny, skinny and dummy. These hurtful words I heard pretty much on a daily basis. They were as bad as the physical hitting, pushing and the odd kicking that I received while growing up. Words do hurt! They hurt and burrow themselves into our minds, bodies and souls and become a part of who we think we are. They mold and shape us and they become our own belief patterns that we believe to be true as children, teens and even adults. Hurtful words and abuse seem to strike us even harder when they come from the very people that we love and look up to.

I suffered this torment almost daily from my older cousin Jake, who is only three years older than me. Jake, came to live with my family as a baby, and being that he was already there when I was born, I thought of him to be more of my brother than a cousin. I knew and understood that most siblings fight, but why did Jake, who when I was four, all of a sudden turn on me? Why did he go from being my friend and playing with me to hurting me so much? And, even more so, why was it that the more I tried to get him to like me again, the worse he would treat me?

Before this torment, I remember playing cars and trucks with him, and playing outside in the back yard. He was one of my only friends, as I did not go to school yet and I only had a couple of neighborhood friends. I looked up to him, and to me, he was the greatest person out there. I think a part of me even wanted to be just like him, as I was more of a tom boy than a girly girl. Then one day, at the age of four, everything seemed to change. Jake never wanted to play or hang out with me anymore, instead he dreaded me. He seemed to hate me and he started to become mean and abusive. If he did ask me to play a board or card game with him I was more than willing, because I wanted him to like me again. But I learned, quite quickly, just to let him win, no matter what. He usually did, but the odd time I would win, meant being called more names, wrecking the game and me having to pick up the pieces or, worse yet, getting punched. I did not want to tattle on my cousin, because that meant he may get into trouble and I would feel extreme guilt. I think, in my mind, I thought it was because I must have done something to deserve this treatment, plus tattling would mean that he would hate me more.

I feared coming home after school the days that my Mom and Dad worked, because we would be alone and that meant no one was there to prevent it. Sometimes it would even be him going into my room, wrecking my posters or stealing my babysitting money or Halloween candy and other times, most times, it was him being verbally, emotionally and physically abusive. All of this physical, verbal and emotional torment continued until I was about fourteen. Maybe things changed, because at this point I had a boyfriend or because my cousin's friends would comment to him about his behavior towards me. A few of his friends, as adults, have since told me how bad they felt for me, as Jake's hate towards me was well known by our friends. After the age of fourteen, Jake just ignored me. He would only acknowledge me when he needed to borrow money, which he never paid back, or if he needed some kind of favor, which of course I was still more than willing to do as this may be the time that he would like me and we would get along again. I even remember begging God to get Jake to like me; I just didn't know what I did wrong. Looking back, this seemed to consume a lot of my young life.

My cousins' abuse and ignoring me was to become the new normal pain that I would feel for many years to come. Even harder for me was that my cousin was a nice guy to everyone else. I saw him help others and go out of his way to help kids who were the underdogs at school. He was well liked and had a kind heart to everyone else and he continues to be to this day. So, again I would think, why not to me?

I had a lot of self- hate due to a low self esteem in my teens. I guess anyone would when they constantly are getting abused and constantly hear how horrible, ugly, stupid and scrawny they are from someone, who is supposed to love them. The mean words were now also my own words I would say to myself, they became who I thought I was. This self- hate was starting to affect my school work and friendships. I didn't have a lot of friends and the ones I did have always seemed to turn on me. I honestly think I only had one true friend, who I am blessed to still have in my life. I was a quiet, shy, sensitive and very insecure young girl.

I had an incident when I was 13, where all of my friends turned on me and life seemed that much worse; it just seemed that I had a lot of bad events happen to me and I could not understand why. I began to dislike life and I just wanted it all to be over. One day I stopped at the store on my way home from school and bought a bottle of aspirin. I went home and swallowed each and every pill from that bottle. I was in tears, feeling so helpless and sad, I was thinking about how I just didn't want to feel miserable anymore, I didn't want to feel anything, I just wanted it to all go away. I remember lying there for a while with the aspirin in me, and then, I heard this whisper. It was a gentle whisper that told me to "tell your Mom." I remember her coming home from work minutes later and me not wanting to tell her what I had just done. But the whisper continued and I knew that I really didn't want to die. I just wanted the bad feelings to end, so I got up and with a lot of guilt and shame,

3

I told my Mom. My poor Mom, what a nightmare to know that your daughter just tried to end her life, the pain and guilt, as a mom for not knowing what was upsetting her daughter. She drove me to the hospital. Thankfully the aspirin was not in me long enough to have done too much damage, other than the emotional damage I must have done to my parents.

I think everyone just thought it was all for attention, and, in a way, it was. I think I was begging, on some kind of level, for someone to notice just how sad I was, how much emotional turmoil I was in. You see, on appearance I looked happy, I was the people pleasing girl that everyone thought to be happy, friendly and always smiling. No one saw my pain, my anger and self- hate, and no one really knew why.

I don't recall anyone being too concerned about my suicidal attempt. No one really sat down with me to see what was going on in my world that would make me do something so extreme, and so life resumed back to how it was. I guess I became numb and just learned how to block out my feelings even more than before, and that led me to add that much more armour around myself.

The rest of my teenage years were quite reserved. I had a high school boyfriend whom I spent most of my time with. Other than him I didn't have many friends and now looking back, I held the few friends I did have at arm's length. I think I was too scared of not fitting in and having everyone turn on me again, and so my armour was built up, that much more, out of fear of getting hurt.

At the age of seventeen, I unexpectedly got pregnant and had my oldest son, Justin. I don't condone having a child so young, but he truly was the best thing that happened to me and he made my world look so much brighter. The love that I had for him was so intense and so strong, that for the first time, I was truly happy. He made me want to be the best that I could possibly be, both as a mom and as a person. I never once regretted having him at such a young age, as I believe that, in many ways, he saved me both then, and again, a few years later.

In 1994, I met my ex-partner, Greg. I was already a single mom to my oldest son, Justin, at this time. Greg was a couple years older than me and a farmer with the strongest shoulders and arms that I had ever seen on a man. I thought of this as true strength and I fell in love with his attitude and ability to tell people what he thought, good and bad, without hesitation. He did so in such a way that people were careful and treaded lightly around him. For me, telling someone what I truly thought was terrifying. I could barely even express myself, never mind tell people what I thought in an angry way, as good girls don't raise their voice, get mad, speak their truth, or so I was told or somewhat thought. In my insecurity, I saw this in Greg as powerful; now I understand that people act like this to guard themselves, it is their way of protection, it's their own armour. They think that by doing this no one will see their pain, their vulnerability and they won't get hurt.

I thought I was so lucky to have this man in my life. I was so naive, in spite of what everyone else knew and I couldn't see that our relationship was getting bad. It too was abusive, physical at times in the first few years, but again, the emotional and verbal abuse, throughout the years I was with him, was to be what struck me the most. Things continued to get worse; I was again really starting to think that life was horrible. I remember one incident when Greg punched me so hard, I fell to the floor where he started to kick me, he was yelling some mean things which caused more pain than the physical abuse, and the saddest thing was that the next day in my insecurity; I was the one apologising to him, for my rude behaviour. I thought the whole incident was my fault and because I didn't want to lose him, I apologised. (This resembles the same behavior as with my cousin Jake)

The last time he was physically abusive was a night after a friend's house party. We arrived home and were arguing, when he reached out and started shaking me quite hard. He grabbed me by the neck and proceeded to choke me. I passed out. I eventually came to and was mortified. I did not know what to do. The man that I loved wholeheartedly just treated me like I was nothing, like I was nothing important to him. I knew I should leave him, but I was far too insecure and afraid. I knew that I needed to get out of this toxic situation and started to look at leaving, but a week later I found out I was pregnant with our son Devin.

It was hard enough when I was a single mom with Justin, and had no idea how I was now going to be able to do it with a new baby. So, I stayed with Greg. Thankfully the physical abuse stopped but the emotional continued, and it was to get much worse as time went on. In his eyes, I could never to do anything good enough, and I can now only assume, that he, himself was not feeling good about himself and he turned his pain out onto me. I think, because I was used to this behavior from my childhood, I felt that it was somewhat normal, and it was easy to block most of it out or shut it off. It was like I kept adding more armour around myself and somehow, on some level, I believed that I still deserved it all, that somehow I was not good enough and this was just how it was to be.

One reason on top of me thinking that this abuse was my fault and why I stayed with Greg is that I could see through his armour. I have many spiritual gifts that I was born with, in fact, I believe that we all have them and I will share, as you read on, some being sensitive, empathic and intuitive. Another gift that I have is that I can sense and sometimes see people on a soul level; I can sense and see their soul. Everyone on a soul level is beautiful, sensitive and caring and although Greg was abusive, his soul was absolutely beautiful; it's just that he was hiding it under all of his own pain and armour, the armour that he built up around himself.

This was so confusing to me, at the time, because as bad as things got, I could feel his beautiful soul and so I clung on to hope, hope that maybe one day he would let his guard down, take off his armour and become who I felt his soul to be. I remember crying a lot and thinking "why did all of this pain and abuse have to happen to me?" Why did my partner treat me so badly, when I was trying so hard to be the perfect woman for him? I thought if only I cooked better, kept the house spotless, and was prettier, sexier, and if I did as much for him as I could, then maybe he would see how much I loved him and he would love me more. I knew he loved me, in his own way, as there were some good times, but as I look back now, they were few and far between. I was now at my worst low point and was thinking, "Why, when I tried so hard to be a good person, did life seem to get worse?" I really started to hate myself again. I was sad at whom I was, and I said a lot of mean and hateful things to myself. I would look into the mirror and only see all of my ugliness; not so much my appearance, but my inner turmoil. I hated myself and thought I must be this horrible person, who just didn't matter. It was like Greg took over for my cousin. I had no idea, at the time, that all the negative things I was saying internally to myself, was happening to me externally. All of those means things, that I was feeling and saying to myself, were actually happening to me from Greg, because that's what I believed and felt about myself.

During that time, Greg, was my mirror, showing me how I was, in fact, treating myself. I was allowing him to treat me that way, because I was allowing myself to treat me that way. It would take a few more years for me to be open to and understand this concept, let alone come to understand and know that we are the creators in our own lives and I was creating all of it. All of the mistreatment I was receiving was the effects of how I was actually mistreating myself, mainly because I hadn't healed or dealt with the previous pain due to my cousin, and other childhood issues. I was unconsciously recreating the same patterns, and I was the one actually doing it all to myself, with my own thoughts and feelings, not intentionally, but on an unconscious level it was my own doing. This was a hard pill to swallow, and I didn't want to believe it. Who would want to believe in such things? But, in time, I came to understand, and fully believe, this whole new concept, and this concept led me to be able to heal.

Chapter 2
Slowly, my healing begins, as well as rediscovering my spirituality

I began trying to heal, or looking back, I just knew that I needed to do something to feel better. I started thinking that I needed to go back to church, hoping this would help me to be a better person. To be a better person would help fix everything, right? Or so I thought. After all, I thought I was pretty nice to others and trying so hard to be "good", but I was not attending church, so this was what I thought was part of the problem. I thought maybe because I had become so distant from God that maybe going to Sunday services was the missing link and that He could help.

I attended Catholic school, up until grade eight, and as grateful as I am to have this part of my path to finding some spirituality, I questioned most of what was being taught to me. I remember being told that God (this man in the sky with a long white beard) made me and that He loves me unconditionally, but He will send me to hell if I am bad, and that God sees everything that you do so you better be good. If he loves me unconditionally, than why should I worry about being so bad? I was taught to live in fear, and as frightened as I was for hearing this, this did not make sense to me or that Jesus died for my sins. If he died for my sins, then why should I fear going to hell? After all, my sins were wiped clean because of him, were they not?

I questioned the church's teachings, as well as my own intuitive being, but because of my intense fear of being bad and going to hell, I just kept it all inside of me and learned to not even speak of it. I grew to have intense fear and this fear kept me from finding who I really was. I knew I was different than my peers, in the sense that sometimes I could feel their emotions or know what they were going to say before they said it. Like I mentioned earlier, I could sense and sometimes see people on a soul level and was confused to what that meant. Like the time my friend laughed at me, because I said I could see air. I thought that everyone could see air? I later found out that it was energy, the vibrations of energy around people or even a room where a person may have been in. To me it was air. I can describe it as small flickering dots, almost like a mirage, that flicker really fast when someone is high vibrational. This rapid flickering means that someone is happy, positive, and spiritual, and has worked on healing themselves. If I am around someone who is depressed, negative, mean and still in a state of being a victim to their own circumstances, they are low vibrational and this energy is very dense and moves at a slow pace. I have come to understand that we all have a vibrational frequency; each individual person's is unique to them. All of our conscious and un-conscious belief patterns, everything that we think and feel about ourselves and think about our outer world is part of this frequency. The more healing you do on yourself, the more positive, loving, self respect and respect for others and the more aligned with your soul you are, the higher this vibration is. Some may call it an aura or our energy field.

I also had a sense of deceased people and dreams that would come true. I had this deep sense of knowing that there was so much more to God than what I was taught in school. By certain sensations in my body, I also had the ability to tell when someone was lying to me. I was told through religion class that all of this was bad, that it was evil and that God puts people in hell for these kinds of things and this was Satan trying to get to me. So, out of severe fear, I shut this part of myself off. I tried to ignore it and not be so "weird", because who wants to go to hell? Or be weird in front of your friends? Definitely not me, I just wanted to be a good girl, have people like me and, above all, to be normal.

And, so again, in my mid twenties I attended church, and enjoyed the sermons, music and some of the people that I met, and I helped in the daycare room and started volunteering on Wednesday nights with the youth program. I even had Greg attend services, as well as a few courses the church offered on bettering ourselves. A few years of this and I still was not feeling any better, life still looked the same as it did before. In fact, it started to feel worse. I could still not understand why, but obviously church wasn't doing it for me and one of the last sermons I attended was all about how this "new age" religion was the work of Satan. This upset me again as I knew that I was what he considered to be "new age". My Mom had a wonderful saying that I like to use, she would say "people go to where they are fed." Meaning that it doesn't matter what church you attend or what spiritual books you read, what matters is that you do what feeds your mind and soul on a spiritual level, and go to where you feel that God's message feeds and feels right to you. So because I wasn't being fed at this church and it was not feeling right, I stopped attending and kept trying to find out why I could not feel true happiness.

I even went to the doctor for help as my hormone levels were all over the place. I was almost hoping this was the reason I felt so horrible. I tried hormone pills and even a brief time of anti-depressants, but they too didn't do anything, so I went off of them. I came to the conclusion that I was just messed up and that I was just going to have to finally accept it. I also started to get a lot of anxiety attacks and would wake up in such a panic; I had no idea that my soul was begging me to start healing. You see, our emotional pain, if not dealt with soon, becomes our physical pain. Our emotions, if not healed will manifest into physical pain. If we shut off the feelings inside, the feelings manifest into physical pain on the outside. So, in a sense my hormone issues were in fact another reflection of me not treating myself very well. They were the manifestation of me speaking harsh to myself, as well as the reflection of allowing myself to be disrespected by Greg and others.

I remember one night, at the worst I had ever felt, I was sobbing uncontrollably and begging for this God to help me. I just wanted to feel better. Many thoughts of suicide were to again creep into my mind, "how can I make it look like an accident?" I just couldn't take this unhappiness that was controlling so much of my life. Anyone who would have known me at the time would never have thought I was so unhappy. Like my teen years most people still saw me as bubbly, friendly, so nice and above all pretty. Again I was still trying to get them to like me. No one would have guessed just how opposite I felt. It is amazing how we can hide so much of ourselves behind a smile, even an unhappy, fake one.

The day I started to change was when my youngest son, Devin, had come in my room and saw me crying on my bedroom floor, yet again. This was becoming normal. I felt so bad for him, seeing me like this, and I knew I needed to change, to get better at least for my two sons, whom I loved so much and would do anything for. I was so sad and now extremely angry; I had so much anger and frustration in me, more because I just didn't know what was wrong or how to fix it. I asked God to help me to find myself and help me to be happy, I begged Him to help me find out why I felt like this, why it was getting worse and, above all, how do I make it better?

Chapter 3
The answers you seek are already within you

I am not sure of the exact timing afterward, but I kept sensing this voice inside of my mind, the voice that I had ignored for a very long time, many years actually. It was more of a subtle, gentle whisper inside me, telling me to meditate. "Meditate?" Like those monks who sit crossed legged and chant "ohm"? This was part of all that evil stuff from before, the weird stuff that I was avoiding, because I didn't want to go to hell. This was nothing that I thought of doing before, as it was nothing I even knew how to do, but the voice became almost a nagging. It would not leave me alone, so I thought I would give it a try. After all, what do I have to lose? If I was going to hell then hell may be a better place than this sad, unhappy place I was already in.

I remember going to my room and this time, instead of sobbing, I sat down on my floor, closed my eyes and took a breath, and just let myself 'be'. I didn't feel the need to chant, but to just sit and be. It didn't take long until I started to feel differently. I felt tingling sensations run through my body and saw slight visions, which did not scare me as I had this happen several times just before I fell asleep at night, but never thought much of them. I think I thought it was normal before one nods off to sleep as who talks about visions, sensations and bright colors happening before sleep?

My eyes closed, and sensations in my body and visions in my mind's eye. It felt good! I remember feeling a peaceful feeling. I just sat there and enjoyed the experience. This, too, was the first time I felt a real connection to one of my spirit guides. We all have them. We have several, who are always here for us, when we ask. They come along with us on our life long journey to guide and protect us. They want to communicate with us, but it is us, who needs to learn how to become aware of how they guide us and protect us. We need to be open to listening to them, as well as our own little, gentle voice that we all have inside us. I think a part of me always knew my guides were there, but it was at this time that I saw the one who is closest to me. I saw him in my mind's eye. He just smiled at me and told me that he was here to guide me. I have to admit that, as wonderful as things seemed, it also seemed very weird. I even thought that maybe I was just daydreaming or, worse, finally lost my mind all together, but the peaceful feeling I had was enough for me to not really care and to now open to this possibility of spirit guides. After this experience, I found books on psychics and their experiences, what happens to us when we die, and many other related topics regarding spirit guides, mystics and spirituality. I couldn't get enough, until Greg, told me, repeatedly, that I was strange and reading too many weird books. It was bothering him and so, again, I shut it down. I was beginning to think he was right, as I wondered who else I know connects with spirit guides. It took another year, or so for me to go back and try meditating again, as not only was it such a good experience, but I was starting to feel some peace from it.

So, at about 30 years old, I was having a few experiences while meditating. I was now connecting less to my spirit guides, but listening to my own intuition, to my Higher Self which is really my Soul, I now call it my Guidance system. But back, then I couldn't figure out what it all was. At the time, I only seemed to connect when I was really upset or gave myself the time. I didn't dedicate myself as often, because like most women, I worked, was a dedicated mom running kids to and from school, sports, friends' houses, homework and many other things we moms do. I barely had any time for myself, let alone go sit quietly and meditate. Which now, I understand was something I should have given myself the time to do, as one should never have an excuse to not dedicate time for oneself. You are the only one responsible for you and by giving yourself this quality time will actually benefit your family as well. It makes you more peaceful which will in turn bring more peace to your family. Giving yourself time out from the constant daily routine will show the Universe that you are taking care of you and then you will get back the same in return.

I then had what was to be one of the first of many big experiences that I have had. Just shortly after my cousin Jake was up to my parents' for a visit, his usual ignoring me was really starting to bother me again. I couldn't figure out why it was bothering me, as I was so used to it, and I even once meditated on forgiving him for all of the pain that he caused me. I thought I was good with it all, but apparently I was not. I was babysitting my niece, Angela, who is the same age as my youngest son, Devin, and they were fighting. She was tattling on him, for something that he had done, and my response to her was, "Angela, Devin is just a little boy", and before I could finish responding, I had this 'AHA' moment or this thought that came into my whole being. I thought about how I had forgiven my cousin, as a man, for all of the hurtful things he had done, but never forgave him as the little boy.

That night I did a mindful meditation. To me, a mindful meditation is when you pick a topic, usually an event that happened to you, and you bring yourself back there and heal it, as best as you can. You don't have to relive it, but as hard as it might be, just bring the feelings that you felt at the time and try to understand and heal

14

them. So, in my mindful meditation, I brought Jake and myself back to an event when we were little, where he is calling me names and I kept telling him that I forgive him and that I understand that he must be, for some reason, in a lot of pain to want to hurt me so much. I have come to believe that people, who are hurting inside, turn and hurt others… hurting people, hurt people. His own inner pain came out and he took it out on me. I forgave all the times that he hurt me and had asked him why? (Again, this was done in my mind while meditating) This was the moment where everything started to make sense. My mind brought me back to the day of an event that even though I remembered. I tried to ignore and put it somewhere else, somewhere deep in the back of my mind. I buried it away so as not to have to think of it ever again. I tried so hard to ignore it that I had no idea this was to be the reason that started the journey for me to feel so unhappy.

The moment when everything changed and the day my cousin, my best friend, started to hate me. I was about four years old playing in a neighborhood friend's back yard. Jake came up to me and told me that one of our neighbors's, had some candy for me. We didn't get candy much as kids, so I was more than exited to have some given to me. I remember thinking about which kind and color the candy was going to be, hoping it was red my favorite color. I walked up the steps with Jake behind me, I was sure that he was excited to get some candy, too. Our neighbor was at the door, welcomed us in and led us down the hallway to his bedroom; I had a feeling of "this does not seem good", almost like something bad was going to happen. The neighbor told Jake to wait at the opened doorway of the bedroom and then he proceeded to undress me and put me up on his bed where he sexually molested me. My young mind knew that what he was doing was wrong. I remember knowing that this guy should not be touching me, he should not be doing the things to me that he was doing. I was so young that I did not know what to do. I just remember lying there kind of frozen, and when he was done, instead of candy, he placed a bunch of pennies in my hands. I remember the confusion of no candy and the sickening feeling I had in my stomach from the events that had just happened. I walked up to Jake, who knew what was just done to me, and who also was just given some money by the neighbor. We walked out of the house and went home. This is where I now realize just how bad one horrible event can mold and shape you for the rest of your life, it changes every part of you and makes you believe in many, many negative limited and not so real belief patterns. Although I have to admit that the sexual abuse was bad enough, it was all of the events to happen afterward, that damaged me the most. They were to become the patterns that continued to be created over and over in my life, until I could fully understand and heal them.

While in meditation, in this memory, all I could think was "my poor cousin." I could almost feel his guilt for bringing me to the neighbor's house and my cousin's confusion as he could not comprehend, in his little seven year old mind, what was happening to me. I could feel and sense Jake's guilt of not doing anything to help me or to stop what was happening to me. Jake now had all of this guilt and confusion to deal with and this is when he turned his confusion and guilt into to anger toward me. I am sure that he could not understand what was also happening to himself. Even though he did not get abused, in a sense he was, as the effects would be as bad for him. All of Jake's anger and confusion would turn into hate towards me, abuse towards me; his inner pain was so much for a seven year old to deal with. His only outlet was to take his confusion out on me. No wonder he started to act differently towards me and the saddest thing is that no one, but the two of us, knew what happened that day. I thought for sure that I told my Mom and Dad, but it took me many more years to find out that they had no idea; they knew nothing of the events that happened that day.

At home, my Mom saw the money that the neighbor had given Jake and me, and I remember her asking us where we had received it. I told her who gave it to me, but I don't recall if I told her why and what he had done to me. She immediately went and asked my older sister, who was eight at the time, if the same neighbor had ever given her money, and she said that yes he had. Now my Mom was questioning my sister as to why he gave her money and my sister told her what happened to her. It was the same as what happened to me. My Mom stormed over to the neighbor's, threw the pennies into his face and called the police. The police came over to our house and all I can remember is how everyone was so worried about my sister, making sure she was okay. Why didn't they care about what the neighbor had done to me? This became the other big reason for my turmoil; first I am sexually violated at such a young age, my cousin who's like my brother now hates me and I have come to believe that I am not as good as my sister. I am not good enough. My little four year old mind now saw that my sister was more important and that I didn't matter. I was forty- two before I found out that my parents had no idea that the neighbor molested me that day, and I saw their pain when they realized that I felt unimportant, not as good or, not good enough as a young girl, which of course I carried into my adulthood. You see, back in those days, the doctors told my Mom to take my sister home and never talk about the incident again, act like it never happened. So, Mom did just that. Back then, she assumed that doctors knew what was best and, so, it was never discussed.

Unfortunately, I was to be sexually molested and violated again, four more times, by four different men, at the ages of nine, twelve and twice at thirteen years old. I never told anyone. Through my healing process, I realized that at those times, I thought that it didn't really matter, as nothing was done for me from the first incident. I remember that I would minimize it in my own mind and, somehow, I thought that maybe I was to blame, even though I did not consent to any of it. This was almost what I thought life and men were about, as it kept recurring and became a belief pattern in my mind. I do know that it, too, was to become a part of my confused and suicidal thoughts as a teenager, as I remember having a lot of fear, anxiety and confusion from these incidents. How could I not? I was much too young to have these adult situations happen to me, I was forced into something that my young mind could not comprehend. I was forced into situations that were not for someone so young to deal with.

The incident, when all of my friends turned on me and I attempted suicide, was mostly to do with all the pain of these incidences, the confusion in me, and an incident that happened to me at 13 due to a friend's brother, who tried to rape me. I was 13 and he was 23. My friend told everyone that I had slept with him and I was targeted as a slut. Now I realize she, on some level, was trying to protect him. I, of course, did not have sex with him, he tried to force himself on me, but it did not matter, everyone believed her. So again, even though the sexual violation was bad enough, it was to be all of the incidences afterward, with my friends and school peers, that damaged me the most. Their hurtful words and actions towards me were so painful, and the fact that no one believed me, was too much for me to handle. This on top of everything else, made me want all of the pain to end.

I now know and tell anyone, male or female, who has been through something similar, that any act of sexual violation is wrong, no matter what. Especially at such young ages, it is wrong for anyone to do or even say anything sexually inappropriate to you, and to please get help, talk to someone, as you deserve to be heard, as well as healed. Do not minimize or make the situation to be your fault.

What I have come to learn is that if we don't heal from an original situation, it will continually show up in our lives. It shows up to teach us that we are still holding onto the negative energy and thoughts around the main issue. The un-dealt with energy, thoughts, belief patterns and feelings will continue to manifest similar circumstances. In my case, the fact that I did not heal from my first sexual molestation, kept recurring. If I would have been able to heal from it years prior, at the age of four, I would not have had it happen to me again and again and again. This is why it is so important for us to heal from our childhood incidents and to be able to talk and feel safe, to be able to talk to someone, anyone.

So now, realizing all of this through meditation, I knew I had a lot of healing to do and I was going to do everything I could to heal, first for myself and also for my boys, who were, and still are, the most important people in my life. It was hard, at first as I had no idea how I was going to do this, but I knew that if I kept meditating, listening to my intuition and guidance that I would eventually figure it out.

I started doing as many mindful meditations as possible. Sometimes I would go back to a scenario over and over to fully release it, like when I was forgiving my cousin in my previously mentioned mindful meditations.

Other times, I would allow myself to get mad and even yell at him in my mind's eye. I would tell him that I was mad at him for hurting me, but I would never allow myself to stay upset because I knew it was not healthy and would only create more upset. I would also picture and try to feel a loving energy surround us both. I would do this until I felt the anger inside of me release, and then I would forgive him.

I also found that thinking of myself as a little girl and hugging her was very healing. I would apologize to her for her pain and I would tell her that she has now been heard and that she matters. I would imagine myself hugging her, and loving her. Talking to her as if she was my own child, and in a sense she is, she's my inner child that felt wronged hurt and not heard. I would ask her what she needed from me and I continued to tell her that she is now safe and secure.

Everyone has this inner child. Everyone's inner child is what is in need of being healed, it's this part of us that is still seeking love and acceptance, the part of ourselves that keeps acting out and re-creating events and drawing circumstances to ourselves. Only our adult selves can truly heal this part of us. No one can come and save this part of us.

I find that journaling helps. I would start writing how things made me feel, what I thought the root cause may be. I would write my feelings or what I thought I was feeling, as I was blocked for so long to feel much of anything. I am amazed that once I started writing, the words would just start flowing and I would write and write pages and pages. Writing letters to the people who hurt you is a great way to release some of the toxic energy. Even if it's just something that your Mom or Dad, teacher or friend may have said to you that you are still holding onto. Write the letter, as many times as you need to. Try to finish the letters with forgiving the person or people who made you so upset, and then shred your letters if you do not want to keep them.

Breathing techniques were also a tool that I found to be useful. I noticed that when stressed or upset, I would always hold my breath; almost like I was blocking the flow of the breath from getting in and this would cause anxiety attacks. So, when I felt one coming on or that I was getting tense in my body, I would close my eyes and concentrate on breathing, long and deep breaths. I would concentrate on the air as I breathed in and out. If I had more time, I would sit with my eyes closed and breathe this way for as long as I could. Breathing this way helps me to relax and center myself.

Self-talk, done gently, can help recreate your negative beliefs into positive ones. I would repeat over and over to be gentle with myself. If I would catch myself saying something not so nice, I would change it and forgive myself. I started to change the old "tapes" that I was replaying over and over in my mind. Instead of saying something negative, I would change it to something loving and uplifting. This was very hard to do at first as it seemed I only knew how to talk bad and down to myself but in time I was getting better and it was getting easier. I was starting to believe and feel the positive words I was saying to myself, which was now recreating new belief patterns and new tapes.

I have realized just how being in a state of gratitude of everything in my life, even the smallest things, helped me to see just how much

I really do have. I came to understand that if I am thankful for the things I already have then I will be able and ready to receive even more things to be thankful for.

I found that reading inspirational books was very helpful and I would read as many as I could to keep me feeling positive. Some had a lot of information and others only small amounts, but I would try and take away something positive from each one.

I also found that closing my eyes and concentrating on a word would help change my whole energy. If I was not feeling very happy, I would close my eyes and say, "I am happy". If I was not feeling love, I would even just repeat "love" over and over while thinking about the love I do have. "Love, love, love", and before I knew it, I was feeling love.

One of the best ways to heal and shift the negative energy in you is to become aware of how you are feeling in a situation. If you are with someone who angers you, try to observe the anger. Instead of feeling so angry, try to feel love and compassion for them. I guarantee you if you start to change anger into love, you will change your whole world. The struggle you have with that person is really only the struggle you have within yourself. Remember, that they are just mirroring to you, what is indeed going on within yourself.

I think the best advice is to find someone who can help. It took me a long time to find someone who could help me figure out what all of this meant. There are so many people who can help you on your journey to healing. Seek out any kind of therapy, alternative healers or even any therapist who is open minded about healing in a spiritual sense.

I do all of these techniques, to this day, as I still find that they help when things are stressful or I am trying to figure out anything that needs to be unblocked. And yes, I still have times when I feel down or not so gentle with myself, I am human after all. I still slip from time to time, but I now have the tools and my own inner guidance that helps me to bounce back up and know that I brought it to me on some kind of level to still learn from. Plus, I know that even in those times of slipping up, there are actual gifts to help me to understand what I need to learn. One of my favorite sayings is "this, too, shall pass", and it's comforting knowing that this moment will pass and maybe even be forgotten, and I will move on. I also have a few friends, whom I am blessed with, who understand all of these healing techniques and I feel safe to be able to have them validate me.

Chapter 4
The Law of Attraction

A few years later, in my career as a hairdresser, I had bought my own little salon and in so many ways this little salon saved my life! I found 'me', more of my spirituality, the Universe and my Higher Self, my Soul. I started to become more intuitive, more inspired by energy healing and I started to really listen to that little whisper. I could feel my intuition more often and when I listened, it never failed me. My connection to the nonphysical world slowly expanded and I healed most of myself in that little salon space. I even learned how to help others heal from their painful experiences.

A lot of my hair clients were noticing something different in me and wanted to know what I was doing. At times, my clients would be in tears over something that was happening in their life. I would intuitively know that I was to help them and would just start telling them, on an intuitive level, what I thought they were doing to attract the situation to them. I was quite shocked at how accurate I was and really how easy it is for us to fix, when we understand the Law of Attraction.

One of the many books that I read, at this time, was all about this concept of cause and effect. The book taught me that everything we think and feel creates everything that happens to us. Everything! I remembered my oldest son, Justin, once telling me this, many years before I read this book. We were driving to the bank, which happened to be on a pay day. My bank is downtown and parking is hard to find, even on a slow day. Almost to the bank I said, "Oh shoot, its payday. It's going to be so busy and we are never going to get a parking spot." To which Justin replied "Well, you won't get one now after saying that." I looked at him and said "What do you mean?" He said, "Well, if you think negative then things will be negative and if you think positive then things will be positive." "If you want a parking spot then you should think that you will get one." I thought, "Wow, how does he know this and I wonder how true it is?" Little did I know he was one hundred percent right. I started applying this to all of my life and I read many amazing books that helped me realize that all of my intuition, seeing energy, the knowingness that was in me, and my receiving and seeing physical signs from my Inner Guidance and the Universe, were all actually gifts. And, slowly, I learned how to fully embrace them.

We all have this ability and the guidance. You just have to learn how to tap into it all and, most importantly be open and believe, have faith and trust in yourself. This system was created by you, for you to help you. Just try it for a while and see how effective it really is.

Just after I bought my salon, my relationship with Greg was at its worst and I would find myself escaping to my salon to just be by myself. I worked alone and had no staff, so I would just sit, meditate and read before, and after, my clients for the day. I remember reflecting on this relationship, at this time, and was wondering what to do. I asked my Guidance what was the best thing for me. I asked, "How did things get so bad?" "How did I let things just continue as they did?" "Where was my Guidance when things were so bad and why didn't they try to save or help me?" I meditated on these questions and then was given a scene, in my mind's eye. I was shown a deep, dark, narrow well, and I was sitting at the bottom looking up. I could tell that I was crying and scared, and kept wondering how I was going to get out. I could even feel myself, in this vision, getting mad. Mad, because I felt trapped and no one was saving me. I didn't think that anyone even knew I was down in there. Then, I felt this presence beside me, it was my Guide, (again in my vision), and I asked him why it took so long for him to get there and how was I to get out? He then pointed to a ladder on the wall of the well beside me. That is when I realized that I had the ladder to get out, all along. I had the power, but just refused to see it. I was so caught up in my own inner chaos, victimhood and drama that I didn't even know I could get myself out. It was all up to me, I had to be my own saviour. Mediating helped me to understand that the answers we seek are inside of us and that it's up to us to seek them. We are our own saviours.

Shortly after receiving this vision, Greg was gone for a few days, I had a dream where my son, Devin, who was 10 at the time, came up to me and asked "Why are you still with Dad?", and said that he was sad and didn't want to live there anymore. I woke up in sorrow, as I knew, deep down, that it was time for me to finally leave. I think that my 10 year old son was appearing to me in my dream to reflect a part of me that asked myself the same question, almost every day,for the last several years of my relationship. You see, part of the reason I stayed so long in this relationship was fear. I lived in constant fear of not being able to make it on my own, and not able to support myself and my boys. Greg made a point of telling me, often, that I could never make it on my own and I believed it so deeply, it became my belief pattern. Almost weekly, I would wake up in the middle of the night with severe anxiety attacks, and they, too, were becoming normal to me. I had them every time fear crept up: Fear of being a sinner, fear of going to hell, fear of not being good enough, fear of this new spirituality, fear of speaking up, fear of not being able to do pretty much anything, and fear of not being able to support myself and my boys. I once feared every part of life itself.

The very next day, after having had that dream and with the memory of my vision of myself in the well, I decided to leave my relationship. I knew I had to. At this point, I knew, on a spiritual level, that I would get ill if I stayed, I would never be able to fully heal, and it would also be better for my sons. I packed our clothes, a few memorable things, just what would fit the back of my car, and drove into town to my parents' house. This was the hardest thing I ever did, because I still actually loved Greg, and I was sad that I was breaking up our family, but I knew it had to be done.

This was one of the first times that I saw just how things work out when you really listen to your intuition and follow through with it, and how the Law of Attraction works as well as when we take care of ourselves, the Universe reflects back and takes care of us. I was at my parents' house for 2 weeks. I knew, without a doubt, that I was not going back to Greg, but could not stay at my parents' much longer, not that they didn't want us. I knew their door was open to us, but I needed to be on my own in my own space. Justin, my oldest son, moved in with some buddies and now it was just Devin and me. I was thinking that I should look for a basement suite, preferably furnished, as we left the house with nothing but clothes. I had no idea how things would manifest and how this Universe that I was learning about, was real. You see, where I lived was in the middle of a boom and finding accommodations' was very hard and, if you were lucky enough to find something, it cost a fortune.

I mentioned my situation to a friend and she told me of her friend who was renting out his basement suite, that was furnished, and the price was too good to be true. I got her friends number to go have a look at this place. On the way over I wondered about buying a computer, as I had given mine to Justin, and how I needed a bed first and foremost. The owner, Doug, showed Devin and I the basement and it was perfect! I remember seeing the big screen TV and thinking how wonderful it would be to be able to watch what I wanted, something I wasn't able to do much in my relationship. Doug even had an old computer for me to use and a new bed from one of his daughters that she never used. Everything seemed to be, and feel, right, and to just flow and fall into place. As time went on, things slowly kept getting better, but there were still a few more lessons to learn, actually, a few more big ones.

Another lesson my Guidance gave me, when I asked where they were when I felt I needed them, was this, "Would you want your child to always be holding your hand and asking you for help with every little thing that they are doing or would you prefer they empower themselves, by letting go, so they can make their own decisions and do things for themselves?" This is how our Guides are with us as well, they don't just give us the answers. We must learn how to figure out our own lessons, and do the work to seek, so we shall find. This is what gives us our true empowerment and also helps us to connect to our Higher Selves. I have also come to learn that we have the answers, to what we seek, already inside of us. If we are the creators in our own life, then surely we know what the answer to what it is we need.

I have also come to know that with every problem comes a solution. So, instead of worrying about the problem, which will create more problems, start thinking of a solution. Thank the Universe for showing you the solution. The solution will show up. It has to because you willed for it to be so. By concentrating on the solution, you take yourself out of fear, out of worry and struggle. What we resist will always persist.

Chapter 5

What we think about, will always come about.

I began feeling better about myself and my future. I was able to support my sons and myself, and my spiritual side continued to slowly blossom. I started to understand more about the Universe. To me, the Universe is a big energy source that reflects right back to you everything that you think and feel, and it delivers to you exactly what you put out, in one form or another. We attract things to us via the Universe to show us what we are thinking and feeling. A hard lesson in this was a year before I left Greg, I was working in my salon, which was not mine at the time, and someone slipped and fell outside on the ice. It was a day of freezing rain and the owner of the salon, who was not in that day, had no salt to de-ice the walkway. I called the owner and she told me that the rental company deals with that and not to worry. I also called the rental office, only to get their voicemail. So, back to the lady who fell, she decided to sue. Here I was in the middle of a separation and now I was being pulled through a law suit. This was to be the toughest lesson of my life, but just at the time when I had woken up to how we really do create everything that happens to us via our thoughts and feelings.

I was at another low point. Going through a law suit was painful and I kept wondering how I could have created this. If we create everything that happens to us, how on earth did I do this? It made no sense that I would create such a thing and how could I? And then I started to break things down. The lady who fell was supposed to be walking with a cane (support) and she slipped and fell because she had no support. This sounded like my exact words that I thought for years. While thinking of leaving my relationship, the words of "How will I support myself without falling on my arse?" were there. I was so worried about supporting myself that the worry and fear was brought right back to me in the way of a lawsuit. Really? "This was my own doing?" Yes, it sure was. My negative thoughts, and mostly my negative feelings, were sent out to the Universe and delivered right back to me. What we think about, really does come about.

The one good thing about this concept is that as soon as you figure out why you attract the bad events to you, things have a way of working themselves out. I like to think of it as a reward. It's like the Universe rewards us for doing the hard work to find out what we did wrong, in order to heal from the experience and hopefully never do it again. In this case, I was not liable and was wiped clear of the lawsuit. Thank God!! I was now understanding more of the mysteries of the spiritual side of life and how we are all connected, and not just "things happen for a reason", but they happen because of us, to show us what we need to work on to heal. They show us what we are thinking and, most importantly, what we are feeling.

Another great example of how we create events is the time I caught myself complaining to a friend about not getting any child support from Greg. This both angered me and superficially empowered me. Greg often told me that I would never be able to support myself and a part of my empowerment was thinking, "Oh, yes I can support myself and I don't need anything from you." That was also my ego coming out. As I heard myself complaining to my friend, that little voice inside my head said "you should know better." I knew what it meant. It meant that I was creating not getting child support, because that is what I was saying and putting out to the

Universe. It was true, but only because I was making it true. From that moment, I changed my thoughts and words. I started thanking Greg for supporting our son. I would say it to myself every chance I could, especially when I felt anger toward him. "Thank you for supporting our son", "Thank you for supporting our son" and before long, and without me having to ask, he just started giving me a little money here and there. Wow, it really works! I kept saying it as now I saw evidence. The most beautiful thing that happened, as a result of me changing my negative thought into positive, was that Greg and my son, Justin, started talking again after 3 years of Greg not speaking to him. They not only mended their relationship, but Greg started helping Justin fix his truck, get truck parts, go for lunch and hang out. Now he was supporting both of the boys. Now I was starting to change, as much as I could, from negative into positive. If I caught myself being negative about anything, I would change it into a thankful, positive comment.

I could also see how I drew Greg to me. As I said earlier, he was the mirror that was reflecting just how bad I was to myself. The energy from the abuse from my cousin that was not healed, and his abusive words became my own abusive words and feelings I had towards myself. These were being recreated by Greg, and he was to become the actions to my feelings. I was abusive to myself so he reflected that to me. The Universe delivered what I was putting out there. Once I realized this, I promised to never say a mean thing to myself again. You would think that I had a lot figured out at this time, and granted I did, but I still had a long ways to go, and it would take a few more lessons for me to really get the message and just how I may have healed from some past events. But now I needed to fix the new creations I was forming with my thoughts and feelings. I was still not fully treating myself with love and respect. I was getting there but I still didn't fully get it. I did have a lot of great things happening to me during these times, and I was trying to be positive, but for some reason we seem to have to learn the hard way. This is usually because our negative emotions tend to have stronger feelings than the positive ones. I find that anger, frustration and resentment have such intense feelings and, in this intensity, we let it take over, because this is what we put out and what gets delivered back to us. This is why it's so important to learn from the feelings, "Why am I feeling so mad, angry or resentful?", "What are these feelings trying to tell me that I need to work on within myself?"

I started to see and learn that saying positive affirmations really helped me to start to really love myself. I also started to learn how to say "No Thanks," and I quit trying to be such a people pleaser. This, too, was hard, still can be at times, and I had to stop hanging around with people who were not good for me. I had to let go of a few friendships that were either toxic or not in alignment with what my soul wanted. Not that these people were bad or mean to me, but on some level our energies were not mixing well and they, too, were my mirror as to where I was at emotionally and I knew that in order to continue to grow, I had to cut ties, or at least cut back our time together. They, in their victim-hood pain, would drain me of my own energy. It's like they would draw from me my good energy to help them feel better and then it would deplete me.

It took a while to believe in the affirmations, but I would start to tell myself that I was worthy, that I mattered, and that I was important, not in an egotistical way, but in a gentle way. As I put on my make up for the day, I would tell myself "I love you." Some days it worked and others not so much, but I knew that I had to keep trying as something was definitely working.

I made a point of showing myself that I was worthy as actions do speak louder than words, not just to others but mostly for ourselves, and I would be as gentle with myself as I possibly could. I had to be cautious of what I was thinking, feeling and saying to others, about others and, most importantly, to and about myself. If one does not love their self and say nice things about themselves, then how can they toward others? Or better yet, have others say it to you.

We are extensions of God

My meditations are now a part of my daily events and sometimes I just sense this amazing feeling in my body, like I am in the most blissful state, and other times I receive messages from my Higher Self. The best way for me to describe our Higher self is it's our Soul; our Soul is connected to the Universe, to our Guides, Angels, each other and to God. Our Higher Self is the part of us that is an aspect of God, the Creator. My concept of God changed and I was shown God as an Energy Source, not the man in the sky that I was taught to fear. God is not only in us, and is a part of us, but is us. We are all sparks of God and we, too, are an aspect of God, and this energy source is pure unconditional love.

My favorite image on this topic was one day when I was really struggling with the idea that I was an aspect of God. "How could this be?" "I am not an aspect of God!" There is no way possible. I think I was even feeling some fear from Catholic School and the thought of going to hell for even thinking this. In a meditative state, I was shown a massive energy source. It was as far as I could see lengthwise, as big as the sky could be. The color was sparkling blue, purple and silver, it shimmered, and had the most beautiful glow to it. I knew this energy was God. Under this energy, beside me, were hundreds of plants, trees, animals, and people, hundreds of people of every race, religion and nationality. They were all standing with me under this beautiful blue, purple and silver Divine energy, when all of a sudden our bodies, and leaves and trunks from the trees just faded away and what was left were our souls. Our souls were the exact same blue, purple and silver, sparkling energy as God's energy above. Our soul and God, who is energy, are the same. That is when I understood that we are not only all equally one and connected, but that we, too, are extensions of God. We all have this same beautiful, loving energy, each and every single one of us, as well as insects, fish, animals, plants and trees. We are not just here as humans, but as God, spirit, having a human experience. Our God (Higher Selves) want to experience what it is like to be human, as each and every one of us. What an amazing sight I was given and how grateful am I to be given this scene.

I want everyone to know that they, too, are able to be given the gift of being able to get visions. First, you must give yourself the time to be still. You must first allow yourself the time to sit quietly and be open to receiving anything that your Higher Self or your Guides want you to know. This is also a way to show yourself that you are deserving. Give yourself the gift of meditating, you will never regret it. It will change your whole being and way of life.

If you try mediating and you can't seem to focus or your mind wonders all over the place, then try just relaxing at first, close your eyes and enjoy sitting quietly. Try visualizing a favorite spot where you love to be, then concentrate on your breathing and take long slow deep breaths. You can also visualize beautiful colors entering the top of your head and washing down over yourself as you are feeling good, feeling relaxed, happy or whatever feeling you need to concentrate on. Another meditation that I do is, I lie flat on my floor, because I like to feel the ground as it grounds me, and I let myself feel the energy flowing in my body. You can start to do this by just thinking of and feeling your toes, then when you feel the energy in your toes, bring your awareness up to your knees, then your hips, and continue to feel and move upwards. This will help you to concentrate and not have your mind wondering all over the place, as well it will help you to feel the energy in yourself.

Do what feels right to you. Honor yourself, give yourself time and don't give up. I was fortunate enough my first time to receive positive results, but not every time was like that. I had to meditate for a long while before I could clear my mind every time.

Most important, be gentle with yourself. I struggled a lot with being gentle, so, be kind and don't get discouraged if you feel you are not getting anywhere, just being able to sit quietly for a while, will do you good. There are also a lot of different guided meditations that you can find on the internet or buy from local metaphysical stores, which will help a lot as you will have to listen and focus on what is being said.

You can also search for local mediation classes as more are being offered by awakened and helpful people. The most important thing is to trust in your own intuition and listen to what feels right for you.

My vision of God, as an energy source, has also changed on what I call God. It really does not matter on what name we want to give this amazing Creator. I honestly think there is no word to even describe it, as it is as amazing and loving as possible and the energy and feeling is beyond any word that I can even think of. So if I mention God, Divine, Creator or Source, please do not get caught up trying to make a distinction, as they really are all the same to me.

The Lady in the Parking Lot

I wish I could say that, by this point in my life, I had it all sorted out and that I was on cloud nine. Unfortunately, I was still learning all about human experiences and I now had yet another lesson on how I was slightly slipping into old patterns of treating myself.

I am human and definitely slipped into some old patterns with what I was putting out to the Universe via my thoughts and feelings. After a few years of being single, I was in a relationship, the last one I was to be in for many years and it ended abruptly. I also had an important friendship, with someone whom I thought was my best friend, end at the same time. I was starting to get quite hard on myself, not as bad as before, but I was again saying some negative and unkind things to myself. I was at a low point and was borderline verbally abusive towards myself, more because I was feeling lost. I had lost both my boyfriend and best friend. I now understand that both were not good for me. They were toxic on some level and I know that they were never to stay a part of my life. I knew that I drew their energy to me, to see what I still needed to heal within myself. Even with this awareness, it was still hurtful; my ego was more than hurt. This is where I forgot, and almost did not care, about the mirror.

But, as I should have known, I was to get back from the Universe what I was putting out and so my mirror was to show up as an abusive lady who harassed me for quite some time. One day as I was at work, I noticed a lady who had just parked in one of my stalls at the salon that was clearly marked Salon Parking Only! I opened the door and asked her politely to move to the visitors parking stalls and before I knew it, she was calling me names, insisting that she can park wherever she wants, as her daughter lives in the apartment building that was directly above my salon. I told her that I pay for those spots and they are not for tenants or their guests, but she continued to swear at me. I told her that "I would call a tow truck if she did not move," all the while I was nervous, as I am not one to engage in confrontational incidences.

She lived out of town and came to visit her daughter every few months and when she did, she would either park in my spot or throw garbage off of her daughter's balcony which would land at the door of my salon. Once she dumped her ashtray in front of my door and another time she dropped a large sheet of glass that shattered in front of my salon. When she would walk up the walkway to the entrance of the building, she would walk slowly, stop and stare into my shop, and just glare at me for no reason. This continued and finally I called the office of the building in which I rent my salon. I told them what was going on, but a few more incidences where to happen. There were more of the same types of things, but her favorite seemed to be that she would just park her car in my stall and sit in her vehicle, smoking her cigarette, almost daring me to come out for a fight.

I had enough. This was starting to affect my business and I was ready to find another location for my salon. I went to the office and told the manager that I would not be renewing my lease, as this lady was harassing me too much. The manager asked me to please stay and that she would look into it. She later called to tell me that she had given them a warning and the next time anything happened, the lady's daughter would be evicted. This, of course, angered the lady, who proceeded to tell the office manager that she had rights and that she was some important person who works for a women's shelter in another province. This is when it all made sense. Here was this woman, who works for abused women, showing up and abusing me. She was reflecting me and how I was slipping into old patterns of verbally and emotionally abusing myself. The lady was my teacher, my mirror, showing up at the perfect time to help me to understand what I was doing, and I should have known better.

It makes me sad to think that she was harassing a woman and at the same time working with harassed women in a shelter. I am going to guess that maybe she, too, had a lot of lessons to learn. Maybe she had been abused and her pain was acting out as anger, like an angry, little girl whose only power is coming from a place of her ego and feeling powerful in hurting another.

If we only knew just how powerful we really are with our thoughts and feelings, we would never say a mean or negative thing again, not to ourselves or another. We don't know what another person is going through, and we have no idea what pain they carry inside of themselves.

May you sit quietly and listen to the gentle voice inside yourself, may you see the signs that the Universe is reflecting in you, the messages, coincidences, the serendipities for they are there. They are showing up at the perfect moment to guide you, for the Universe conspires with us through each word, each thought and each feeling. Look and you shall find, listen and you shall hear, believe and it shall be yours.

Paige Orion

Chapter 6
REIKI

Some years prior, I heard about Reiki, (pronounced as ray-key). Reiki is a gentle, non invasive form of alternative healing. It helps one heal on a physical, emotional and psychological level. It is usually done while a person is lying down on a table and the facilitator places his/her hands just above or gently on the client's body. The facilitator uses life force energy, that they have been attuned to in a Reiki class, to assist one to heal and to unblock and balance one's chakras or to bring calmness or a sense of wellbeing. This energy runs through all living things and is used to support, nourish and help one to heal.

Chakras are energy vortexes, like disks that spin in areas of the body. We have several of them, but Reiki concentrates on seven main ones that run up the spine to the top of the head. The first is the Root chakra, located at the base of the tailbone; the second is the sacral chakra located in the lower abdomen; the third is the solar plexus chakra located in the solar plexus; fourth, the heart chakra located in the chest; fifth is the throat chakra located in the throat; sixth is the third eye chakra and located on the forehead between the eyebrows; and the seventh is the crown chakra located on the top of the head. These chakras are invisible to the eye, but they are very real! The purpose of these chakras is to either bring vital energy into or out of the body, and each chakra is connected to organs, tissues and areas of the inner and outer body. These chakras work in alignment with our thoughts and feelings, and can become either blocked and not receive enough energy, or be too open and expel too much energy, which over time can lead to illness or disease in the body. If we become blocked, due to our neglected and negative emotions or limited belief patterns, we start to feel pain in our bodies. This pain, due to unbalanced chakras, tells us that we need to heal ourselves. For example, if a person gets a lot of sore throats, laryngitis, or even neck pain, this may be caused from fear of being able to speak up and being heard, and it will cause the throat chakra to become deficient. Or if one is having lung, heart or chest issues, this would be due to a blocked heart chakra, most likely to do with lack of love for oneself, lack of self-acceptance or not accepting others, and even un-dealt with grief can affect this chakra. So, our negative thoughts can eventually become negative pain in our bodies. The pain shows up to tell us what we need to heal within ourselves on an emotional level.

This was all new to me and I had a lot of disbelief around this concept. I have to admit that I was still experiencing some fear about all of this, the Universe, mystery, Reiki, and such, being evil. Parts of me knew it was good. My intuition knew it was good, my Guidance knew it was good, but I still had some old fear that needed to be dealt with. Thankfully, I had the most gentle and loving Reiki teacher who was, by far, nothing to do with evilness. I took a Reiki class and I could literally feel, in my hands, the energy that was emitting or not emitting from the Chakras of others and even myself. I could feel the energy, it was like my hands had a hot prickly feeling or a very cool sensation and at times I could see the energy. I preferred to keep my eyes closed as I was also getting intuitive messages as to why the person's chakras were blocked. I could describe to my clients what they were doing, emotionally, in their life or what childhood issues they had that was creating such imbalances.

This is when my intuition really took off and became very keen. I, at one point, was told by my Guidance, that I was no longer doing

Reiki; I was now doing my own form of intuitive energy healing. To me, the only difference is that Reiki uses healing symbols and I was not using them in my practice, nor was I working on the chakras as much, but now concentrating on the subconscious and unconscious mind. I was also starting to pick up on my clients' past lives, getting messages from deceased loved ones, and receiving confirmation from clients that I was correct on the messages I had for them. I was now able to start telling them how they, too, could heal themselves by doing a lot of similar techniques that I was doing for myself, and by telling them about the law of attraction. I was able to use my intuition, along with my guidance and my client's guides, to see what the root of some of their issues were, where their painful experiences were still allowing their thoughts and feelings to recur, and how to change the way they were thinking and speaking. And, as an empathic person, I could feel a lot of their physical and emotional pain in my own body. As a facilitator, I had to open my heart and send them as much loving energy as possible, which sometimes was very painful for me to do as it hurt me to feel their inner pain.

This technique of healing would also bring me to their little boy or girl self. I could see what events or feel what happened to them to shut themselves off as children. I have come to understand that when we are children and something bad happens to us or is said to us, we start to shut down out of fear. We don't know how to deal with the emotional or physical pain, and so we build up a shield of armour to help deal with the pain. I see this armour as the negative ego, which we unconsciously create to protect ourselves and to not feel our emotions. It is a survival mechanism that carries us through life that constantly brings up the same emotional issues, fears, habits, and baggage until we understand and heal and embrace those parts of ourselves. We must learn to accept the emotions and learn to love them as they are the parts of ourselves that have been hurt and neglected. In my case, every time I was physically, sexually or emotionally hurt, I would shut down out of fear. My little, sensitive self did not know how to cope and so my own negative ego took over my thoughts and behaviors. It becomes the fearful, negative voice that tells us it's all our fault or we are not good enough. In some cases, it can tell us that we are better than we are and we energetically start to build up subconscious armour around us. In my case, my armour would almost suffocate me and take years to undo, and my chakras would become blocked and unbalanced, and I had to slowly work on healing them one by one.

This negative ego not only becomes the negative voice, but more importantly the negative feelings. My whole people-pleasing nature was that ego voice telling me I was not good enough and that I needed someone to like me in order for me to feel worthy. It was that very fear that started taking over. All of my fears were due to this negative voice, and the negative feelings that I thought were my own. It was the voice of my teachers telling me that if I wasn't a good girl that I would go to hell, the voice that told me being intuitive and mystical was wrong, the voice of feeling ugly, and stupid, dumb and scrawny. This is not to be confused with the voice I receive when being guided. One can tell the difference in the feelings and words. The negative ego voice is all about self. It's the "I am so dumb," or "I am un-worthy," or even the "I am so good" or "I am better than." It has a negative vibe to it and can make one feel anxious and fearful. The guiding voice, however, is very loving, a subtle gentle feeling of "you are capable", "You should meditate," "You are worthy." It's a calm, gentle voice. It's almost the visual of the angel on your shoulder and the devil on the other. As I mentioned earlier, we tend to listen to the negative and so, we become all the negative thoughts. These thoughts become feelings and this is what we put out to the Universe and then get back. This then becomes our reality and is what we think and feel life is all about. We keep attracting all of these negative things to reflect ourselves, especially the parts that we need to heal; people and events show up to be our mirrors. For example, if one were to think they were unlovable, they would keep attracting people and events to show them they are unlovable, and over time one's heart chakra would take a toll, get unbalanced and lead to issues in this area. He or she has no idea that if they changed their thoughts and feelings, and started to think and feel that they are lovable, life would change and they would attract people and events to reflect this new way of thinking. It would become their new truth and their heart chakra could become open and balanced. Just think, if we all knew this concept, our lives would be so different. If we attract the negative, then we have the power and the ability to attract the positive, think positive, be positive, feel positive and then receive positive.

Chapter 7
Sometimes our Journey can inspire others

I was now helping others. This felt good, as it made me think that out of my own pain and suffering, came a gift to be able to help others with their pain and suffering. Plus, by helping others, I realized that every single person on this earth feels the same, at one point in their lives, not good enough, not worthy enough, and not lovable. I realized that we each have a story and each one of us has past and present pain that we hold onto, and many of our thoughts and feelings are not necessarily even our own. They usually come from childhood beliefs that we picked up from our parents, siblings, teachers, churches, friends and even the media. I learned, too, that energetically we sense our parents' and siblings' thoughts and feelings, as well, and think they are our own.

I started to also understand the concept of how we absorb other people's energy. When you are around someone who is very negative and always down, you start to feel it, you feel worn out and next thing you know, you, too, are as depressed and negative. When we spend time with others, our energy intertwines with each others, you actually absorb it into your being and they absorb yours. Some years later, I discovered that the times I was at my worst, sobbing on my floor and having suicidal thoughts, these were not necessarily all my own thoughts. I had no idea of what this concept of absorbing energies and, even more, I had no idea that I was empathic. Empathic people tend to pick up other people's thoughts and feelings as well as physical pain quite strongly. Back at the time of my worst emotional crisis, I was hanging around my good friend, Susan, becoming very close and spending a lot of time together. I could tell that after a day or evening of hanging out, I felt different, I felt kind of foggy, my thinking was not quite clear. I would get anxious and felt not quite myself. I started blaming it on all the coffee we were drinking. After all, we would easily drink a pot, or so, between us and I was usually a one-cup-a- day girl. What else could it be? Well, I was absorbing her energy and her vibration level, and hers and mine were not mixing well.

I started to pick up on some of Susan's thoughts and feelings. I thought this was just my intuition, kind of like I was being psychic, and as usual back then, I tried to shut it off because I loved hanging around her. Susan was beautiful, had a smile that was infectious, and you could not help but like her. She loved to party, talk on the phone for hours and get together with anyone, anytime. Little did I, or most of her friends, know the emotional trauma that she was in.

One day, I asked Susan about the thoughts I was picking up, as I knew some of them could not possibly be my own. She confirmed that she was feeling a lot of what I had sensed. She admitted that she was getting help for having suicidal thoughts and relayed a lot of the things I had sensed to her. I still didn't quite understand that it was some of her feelings that I was feeling as my own. So, on top of my own depressive state, I was also picking up her stuff, energetically and it took me years, later while talking to a intuitive healer during a session to realize that this was not all 'my stuff', it was not just me having the suicidal thoughts, but that I was empathic. This all finally made sense, what I sensed from Susan and a lot of my friends in school. I knew and felt things, but was trying so hard to shut it all out and ignore it, as this was not heard of or well known, plus what was known, I was told was bad.

Susan and I were to drift apart. Now that I look back, I think this was the time that I started my own healing, maybe because I was now just dealing with my own issues and not hers, too. We eventually became friends again, but sadly my dear friend, even after a lot of therapy, eventually did take her own life. Her pain was too unbearable to feel any more, and she felt the only option was to end her life. My heart saddens when I think of this and how I wish I knew, back then, all of the things I know now. Maybe I could have helped her more; maybe I could have offered her some guidance. Maybe, by writing my story, I can help just one person have hope and to help themselves to heal. Susan's spirit visits me often. Sometimes she relays a small message and sometimes I think just to say 'hi'. I miss my dear friend a lot, but I also know that she may not be here physically, that she is here, most definitely, in spirit.

I honestly think that being empathic is the hardest of my spiritual gifts, as being empathic means taking on so much of other people's feelings as my own. Sometimes it is hard to take it all in, because it can be difficult, at times, to differentiate what is their stuff and what is mine. If someone I am around is anxious then I will feel anxious, as well. If someone has a sore knee, I too may get pain in my knee and think it's me until I center myself and even ask myself, "is this mine or theirs?" Again, this can be difficult but it is also what I chose to come to earth to be. I most likely chose it for exactly what it is, to absorb and feel other people's feelings, so that I can help be a better facilitator; I can truly and honestly say, "I understand and feel your pain." I do, however, believe that we are all empathic; some people are just more attuned to being so, than others.

I also want to share how we absorb our parents' and siblings' thoughts and energy, as well. Right from conception, to the time we leave the nest and, even after, if we are very close to our parents, we are interacting with our parents' thoughts and feelings. Kids are not just sponges learning at school, but sponges absorbing our family's energy and thoughts. I see this in children coming into my salon with their parents. I can sense what is going on, on an energetic level and understand that the parents' thoughts and feelings can become the kids'. So, in other words, when you have a child who may be acting out and misbehaving a lot, chances are they are picking up your chaotic energy, or both you and your spouse's. If you tend to be an anxious person, your child may be feeling this and because they don't understand what is going on, this energy needs to be released and it does so by the child acting out. When your child is angry, depressed, hyper, maybe having a lot of temper tantrums, it may be a good time to look within yourself and see what part of you that needs to be worked on. Maybe you, too, have inner anger or such that needs to be dealt with.

I understood this concept while doing a healing session on my father. He was brave enough to let me do an intuitive healing session on him and I started hearing, or more sensing, some of his thought patterns and some of his feelings about himself. I was kind of shocked, as some of these were also mine. I asked him about what I was intuitively picking up and he confirmed it. It all made sense! From picking up his thoughts and beliefs, I understood that our parents have even bigger roles than we think, and as children we become their mirrors to reflect back to them these very things.

This is where I was to learn just how much my two sons were being my mirror, especially my son, Devin. I was to learn just how much my own issues were affecting him, on an unconscious level, and that he was reflecting what I needed to still heal in my life.

Our children do have their own journeys and, as I will mention later, they actually choose us to be their parents, as their souls want the lessons that we create for them with our issues. Our children are also creating their own lives, so not each and everything is due to absorbing and acting on our parents' thoughts and feelings. Because we are so close to them and while we live in the same space, they do reflect us more than we realize. Justin didn't seem to reflect me as much while he was growing up, his soul needed more lessons being absorbed by his father. Devin however, was to be more sensitive and absorb more of my issues. I believe that Devin chose this as part of his Journey for his own lessons and to help us both to grow spiritually.

I believe that we choose some of our journey and lessons to learn before we incarnate onto the earth plane, to heal, grow and evolve. I will discuss this concept a little later on as for now, I must finish with my life's events, and how our children are our biggest mirrors and how Devin was to be mine.

Chapter 8
Looking for joy

Devin started getting headaches around the age of twelve. They were subtle at first and I figured he was just going through a growing phase, but as time went on, the headaches became worse. The first year they were on and off, and he tried taking aspirin, but they didn't do a thing for him. I took him for eye exams and doctors' appointments, but nothing ever came of it. Devin's headaches would seem to come and go, they would come for a few weeks, and then he may not get another one for a few months. After about a year and a half, he started to get them almost daily for weeks at a time. As a mother, I just wanted to fix my boy and as an intuitive energy healer, I wanted to heal him. Devin would not have anything to do with my sessions, being at the time, a little too skeptical. I understood his skepticism, as I too was, but now, I have no doubt that it is all real and can work when one is open to allowing.

So, at this point, and for the next three years with a total of five years of headaches, we were at our wits end. I had taken Devin to several doctors all of whom wanted to put him on medication, or anti depressants, as they were to stop the brain from feeling pain. Both Devin and I refused, as we wanted to know the cause of the pain, not numb it. I took him to several natural paths, and each one had a different answer. One said to stop eating wheat, and three months of a strict gluten free diet, he still was getting the headaches. The next one said no dairy, and so on. Still, there was no answer. I knew, on some level, that Devin's headaches were caused by me, but I could not tell what it was. I had no idea what I needed to heal within myself, as I had healed so much from my past. What could I possibly be doing to myself that was being reflected by my son? The frustration was getting so much worse and I, too, was now going to some intuitive healers for answers. I even went to a few psychics, who were usually extremely accurate, but no one seemed to know what was going on. I had a few tell me that it had nothing to do with me, but I knew, in my gut and in my very being, that this was some of my stuff and poor Devin was my reflection.

The headaches were very strange; they were a massive pain on top of his head, not a migraine, so it was harder for the doctors to diagnose. Devin had CT scans, X-rays, an MRI, visits to Neurologists, several chiropractic adjustments, physiotherapy, and different kinds of bio feedback sessions, massages, experiments with different vitamins, herbs and diet changes. This was getting beyond frustrating as Devin was missing so much school, his sports, and missing out on being a normal teenager.

I would cry a lot, as I had no idea what to do. I was lost and getting scared, as Devin started telling me that he just couldn't take it anymore. My Guidance wasn't strong due to my being in another turmoil state and I found myself pleading with the Universe and getting more frustrated. And I was very angry. I was giving up on myself as a healer. If I can't figure out my son's illness and where it was stemming from and where it was stemming from within me, well then, maybe it was time to give it all up. I actually did, for a while, but in one of my frustration, angry stints, I finally came to my senses, as I knew better. All my frustration was being sent out and returned to me as more frustration. I started changing my thoughts and started saying over and over, "Thank you for Devin's healing," instead of talking about his headaches, I asked my family, clients and friends not to ask about Devin's headaches, because even though I knew they were asking out of concern, it just brought up more frustration. "Thank you for Devin's healing"… and after about a month, we finally got an answer. It was the start of the healing Journey for us both.

I received a phone call from another physiotherapist in town. We were told that she was the best and, after being on her waiting list for 8 months, Devin finally got an appointment to see her. The first appointment was more of a consult and the second, a week later, was to be the first glimmer of light. She could tell right away that Devin wasn't receiving enough blood to his head, and his chest arteries were somewhat damaged. She asked if he had ever had a bad fall or blow to the chest area. Devin, in fact had. Just before he started getting these headaches, Devin, and his friend were playing at the park on a swing set and, as boys often do, they were trying to outdo one another. Devin fell off while quite high up and landed on his chest. The impact was so hard that he broke both of his wrists. His wrists were both placed in casts, and after time they healed, but no one thought to look for internal damage. This was now all making sense. Referring back to Reiki and Chakras, arteries are all about joy, meaning that if one is lacking a lot of joy then the arteries become blocked, or in Devin's case, damaged. Devin's fall happened around the time I was going through both the lawsuit and separation with Greg, and sadly my exact words were, "life is bad and non-joyful!" I was so stressed, at the time, that I was finding a hard time seeing joy, so on some level Devin, energetically picked up on this and must have also felt it, and this all manifested into Devin getting hurt and damaging his arteries. Again, our kids reflect us, my poor son. So, this was when I knew I had to start looking for and feeling more joyful.

At this point, I had been single for quite a while, as Devin's headaches were my main concern. Plus, I knew that staying single for a while would help me concentrate on my inner healing. I didn't get out much, not to date and very rarely to hang with friends. I would just work, come home, spend a lot of time by myself, so I made a point of getting out more, and finding new and fun things to do. This was harder than one would think, because there is not a lot for a single woman of adult children to do. I did, however, see that a local, like-minded friend was having a twenty one day Kundalini intensive yoga class, and my intuition kicked in and said "go." This yoga style concentrates on each individual chakras and certain yoga poses to help balance them out. It felt right, so I joined. I enjoyed attending, met some amazing people and honestly didn't think much was happening, with opening up my Chakras to the poses, until the day we did the Heart chakra. We did an exercise, that was more about the breath than any poses, and, just before we started, we were to write on a piece of paper what our intent for healing was. My first feeling was to finally heal any pain and energy that may have been still lingering from my cousin, as he had just been home for Christmas a few months prior, and things were still the same between us. Not only did this bother me, but saddened my Mom and Dad, as well. I wanted it to be finally healed, to never have to work on it again. Halfway through the breathing exercise, while lying on my yoga mat, I felt this toxic ball of energy leave my body. It was intense and a huge release! I could actually feel it leave. I knew that it was all the energy that I was still holding onto, as well as some of Jake's energy. It was gone, finally gone. I just laid there and let the tears stream down my face, which is something I don't usually do in a room full of people that I don't know, but it was so freeing that I did not care.

Three days after this release of energy, I was cleaning up at work after the end of my day and my cell phone rang. I didn't recognize the number, as it was long distance, but felt the need to answer it. It was my cousin!! OMG!! My cousin, the one who had had nothing to do with me, he was actually phoning me for the first time. He didn't even have my number and had to get it from my sister. One part of me was in shock and the other part was thinking, "yes, this is how it all works, you do your inner work, heal something and then you get a reward." My reward was in the form of Jake calling me. He was in town for two weeks and asked if I wanted to go for supper. Go for supper? Of course! How could I not? The next two weeks were wonderful. Jake came over for supper a few times, we talked, found out so much about each other, he brought coffee to me at work, and he even let me do a healing session on him.

This all seemed a bit surreal, as you can imagine, because I was now, finally, having a relationship with my cousin. I won't reveal too much about his session, except that honestly, he had the most beautiful energy that I ever worked with. I was actually amazed and then also shown why everything happened the way it did when I was four. I was shown that on a spiritual level even at the age of four, I created the whole incident that happened, out of the lessons that I had come to earth to learn as well as the energy that was around my family. I will talk of this concept a bit later to help you make sense of it as it is quite hard to understand how we could possibly create such events. Well, it's not like I purposely created the exact event. I did not want such things to happen to me, but unfortunately, I did draw it to myself on a very, very unconscious level. Plus, I was also to be some of my parents reflection on some level, as I mentioned, our kids reflect us.

My whole family healed around this incident of Jake and I finally talking. My parents were happy that their kids were finally communicating, as this had bothered them and brought them a lot of pain, as well. I can't imagine my two boys never talking to each other, as it would break my heart. After having a night of talking with my parents, everything came out in the open. This is when I was to find out that they did not know about the sexual abuse, and that they did not know it happened to me, they thought it only happened to my sister. So, now, all of my belief about not being good enough or not as good as my sister was dissolved, it was just my four-year-old self, who knew no better. Wow!! This is what happens when we open up and have conversations with our family. I encourage everyone, who is still carrying around childhood pain, to talk and ask questions, with your family, even if it seems too painful. This was to be the first time that I can say I felt peaceful. I, now, was at peace.

Another first, at this time, was something my Mom said to me. She had a hard time with my spiritual side and never understood me on this level. Many times growing up, or even in adulthood, she would give me this strange look and almost discourage me from being who I really was. She would even tell me not to talk about all of this, as it may scare people away.

My Mom said, "Paige, I admit that I don't understand the spiritual stuff on your level. I have no idea what you do, but obviously you have a gift and our family would not have been able to heal if it were not for you." I still tear up thinking about that, as this too was a reflection on all of my growth, healing and accepting of myself.

Shortly after, I decided to start dating again. Devin was still getting his headaches, not as severe, but enough that I knew I still needed to work on my heart chakra and be more joyful. I had had a few minor relationships after Greg and although they were decent men, they still had some resemblance, energetic wise, to him, so I knew that I wasn't really ready. After the last relationship ended, I vowed to stay single until I figured out and healed most of myself. I knew I would just keep attracting the same type of men. One of the best things I did for myself was to stay single for a while and search for what I needed to heal. I had been on a local, online dating site for a year and a half, prior to this point. I was on it more for a spiritual tool, using it to show me what I needed to heal on a relationship sense. I wanted to let the men who messaged me be the mirrors of me, so that I could understand what was still going on within me. For example, one man only talked about his ex-wife, so this told me I still had some healing to do around my ex-partner. Another man got quite mad, when I rejected his invitation for a second date, so this showed me that somewhere in my life I needed to work on rejection issues. This process took a while, but I finally figured out I was still rejecting small parts of my healing. One man seemed very needy, which showed in everything he talked about, and that told me that I still had to take care of some of my own needs. I did go on a few dates with a man I had met a few years prior named Mark and he was to show me some bigger things I needed to heal, but they would show up some time later. I could not fully understand what it was that I needed to learn from him, as this was altogether a whole different experience. There was something I was drawn to, the first time I met him years prior and one that would eventually change my life all together...

Using this dating site as a spiritual tool was a fantastic experience and it worked great at that time, but, a couple of years after that experience, I felt ready to date, this time for real. During the two dates that I did go on, I would get this intense fear to run. These men were, by far, not bad or anything. Their energy and personality were actually very gentle, but my logical mind would have nothing to do with them. I figured I was still not quite ready, but also knew that I needed to actually be in a relationship to fully see the mirror and to fully see what I was missing on a healing level. So, I promised myself that the next man I was to go on a date with and felt something for, I would not run, I would try to allow myself to actually be in a relationship, I was now open and ready, or at least ready to see what I needed to see.

No wonder relationships can be hard, as it's another person's energy that we are actually attracted to. It's usually that they have similar issues as ourselves and they show up to reflect that in us. Most people are unaware of this and so they keep attracting the same type of partners to themselves. If only we knew that they are the perfect teachers to show us what we need to learn. Their pain and our pain are actually the same. They may have different issues, but at the core, the energy is the same. We eventually get mad and upset at them for not being the perfect partner. We resent them for not being a certain way. We want them to be a saviour or someone to give us what we cannot give ourselves, only because we, ourselves, are not feeling good enough, worthy enough or not lovable. We hope they will come and love us, sweep us off our feet, and be the one to finally bring us happiness. In truth, if we looked at them as our reflections, we would understand that, what we don't like about them is really what is needed to look at within ourselves. Plus, they help show you where you are at with how you treat yourself.

Until we understand that true love starts with the self, we will never find it outside ourselves. No one will save us until we learn to save ourselves. No one can make us happy until we are happy inside.

Chapter 9
One Shall Not Judge

I see a profile of this man Joe, on the dating site I am on. I know Joe from many years prior and my experience with him was not so good. My memory of him was someone very arrogant and not so friendly, a real player with women. Several years ago, we had run into each other at a bar and he had said a few mean things to me, so with these memories, and past negative feelings about him, I had absolutely no desire to look at his photos or profile, never mind go on a date with him. After about two months of seeing Joe's profile on this site, I sense my intuition telling me to message Joe. "You want me to Message Joe?" I think not! Why would I do such a thing? I refused. This is something I usually try not to do with my own Guidance, but I can still second guess it in my confusion. This is why it is so important to quiet the mind, because our Guidance has a hard time with us if we are in a chaotic state, and we can't hear it through all the mind chatter. In our quiet mind state, we can also learn to see actual signs from our Guidance that help us know if something is meant or not meant for us. When I don't listen, my Guidance will turn more into a nagging, and I will receive negative signs which will continue until I follow through with what I am hearing or sensing. So, I am still refusing to message Joe, but my Guidance, and now the messages, are continuing and getting stronger. "This just can't be", I am thinking. I finally decide, more plead with myself, that I will message him the next day, as I thought I needed some time to think about what I would possibly say to him after all of these years. Well, within two minutes, Joe himself messaged me. I laughed at myself and said "I get it", as I realized that there was to be a big lesson to learn for me, and because I was more than curious at this point, I replied.

Joe and I messaged each other a few more times and then, finally we decided to meet up for coffee. As we were now getting to know each other, I realized just how different Joe was and that, for all of those years, I was still holding onto that judgement. I guess I forgot that most of us do change over the years. Life changes us and can sometimes harden us and make us turn bitter or, in Joe's case, it can soften us and makes us a better person as he was far from the person I remembered him to be. He was now kind, gentle and I think I can honestly say, that he was the first man that I felt I could trust, the first man to show me that not all men are like the men from my past. I also learned a bit more about not being in judgment of myself and my feeling that I could trust him was my reflection back to me showing me that I was now having more trust in the Universe, as well as myself, and that my beliefs about men were now getting healthier.

Joe and I only dated for about five weeks. I learned a lot in this five week period about dating again: how to have some fun, go to movies, out for nice suppers, have someone cook for me for once, hang out by the river, taking the dogs for walks, singing loudly on a weekend road trip, holding hands, that shopping with a man could be a lot of fun, and that I was really enjoying being with a man for the first time in a very long time. But, with all of this enjoyment and new way of being and thinking, I was still not quite "feeling" it. I knew that I wasn't being fair to Joe as he was starting to have strong feelings for me. He was starting to fall in love and I just did not have the same feelings towards him, not enough anyways, and I ended our relationship. And, with my son Devin, my mirror, still having headaches, I knew that I wasn't quite there in the joy department yet.

I am thankful for this experience with Joe as he is far from the person that I remember him to be years ago. Thankfully, we can learn, change and become better, and when we know better, we act and do better.

A few months after Joe and I ended our short relationship, I felt I was on a role with my lessons and teachers. I was learning so much more at this time and thinking I learned what I needed to learn from Joe, I asked the Universe for my next teacher, not sure who or what it would be. I went to bed one night, asking for my next teacher to arrive. I am now manifesting things quite quickly, and woke up the next morning to find a text message from Mark....

Chapter 10
Mark

This, I think, is the greatest experience I have had up till this point. It is the most unusual, exiting, and crazy experience that I have drawn to myself, maybe because it's the newest or maybe just because I now get "it." Or, in this case, that my heart and soul were about to take over.

Mark is the man I talked of earlier, and who has come in and out of my life for the last six years and is someone who has had the greatest effect on me. I met him the night of my girlfriend's birthday, when she and I went out for a late supper. We had a few drinks to celebrate and she decided that she wanted to go to a bar just across the street from the restaurant we were at.

We walked in and started looking for a table. She saw a couple of men that she knew and proceeded to walk over to them to say 'hi'. Out of nowhere, one of the men (Mark) grabbed my hand and just led me to the dance floor without asking. I did not mind whatsoever, as he was cute and I was feeling kind of tipsy. We danced a few slow songs and went back to where our friends were. After hanging out for a while, we all decided to go back to Marks house. We drank some wine, sat in his hot tub and at one point, while I was walking through Mark's kitchen, he grabbed me and started to kiss me. I remember that kiss like it was yesterday. It was electric! Something was completely different about this man. I knew I had too much to drink, but wow!!

After that kiss, the men walked us to my girlfriend's house, just a few blocks away. The guys left and I couldn't help but wonder about him and that amazing kiss. I knew, in my intuition, that I was going to see this man again, but I had no idea that it was to be years later. At first I thought of him a lot, then it became from time to time, and slowly it became much less frequently. I think I even forgot his name.

So, four and a half years after initially meeting Mark, I decided to join the dating site (this was the first time I was on using the site as a spiritual tool). I soon received a message and was excited. I am thinking that this man looks familiar, but wondering more why something inside of me is going crazy, like my soul was doing cartwheels, jumping up and down with excitement.

Soon into our messaging each other, he tells me that I look familiar. At this point I remember exactly who he is; it's the guy from that night, the kitchen, the hot tub, the kiss… that kiss. We reminisce about that evening years ago and decide to meet up for supper the next night at a new restaurant that had just opened up. As I walked in and saw Mark, my heart and soul started going completely crazy! It was so strange to have my heart and soul so involved already. My logical mind was more curious as to what all this was about, as this had never happened to me before. We had a wonderful time, a great supper, great conversation and Mark even gave me a gift, a book on meditations. What a thoughtful, kind man my mind was saying, but it was my soul that wanted to jump across the table and embrace him.

We left the restaurant, hugged and went our separate ways. As I was driving home, my mind was wondering, what the heck! I know my heart and soul are going crazy but, how? Why? I don't even know him; I just had one encounter with him years ago. I am very confused and, against my heart and soul and in my confusion, I decide that I am not ready to date just yet. I sent him a message telling him thanks for the night but I wasn't interested in being more than friends, and made up an excuse of him not being spiritual enough. You see, I was scared, scared of being in a relationship. After my relationship with Greg ended, I vowed to never open up my heart again and here I am with my heart and soul going all crazy and feeling things that I was not understanding. As good as it felt, I knew that I would lose all control with Mark, and so, out of fear, I just stopped anything from going any further. I felt bad for sending that message, actually major regret was to take over, but it was where I was at the time, and I know I was not ready, or so my negative ego voice made me think.

For the rest of that week, all I could think about was him. My mind would not rest. This feeling of my heart jumping up and down was not going away. The feeling that I should not have run away from the situation so quickly, that I should have at least tried, stayed with me. And then... my intuition told me that I would be seeing him by week's end.

The night I knew that we would see each other, I was actually waiting for his text and, sure enough, Mark sent me a text. We chatted for a bit and he invited me to his place. As I drove up to his house, he was watching for me in the front window and that was when my heart felt light, open and again excited. My logical mind was trying to blame it on the fact that I have been single for so long, but my soul was saying "No, just hurry and get in the house." We talked, drank some wine, and then we kissed. That same electric feeling was back! My whole body felt it, even stronger than before, and this time we made love. That night that electrifying feeling was tenfold, running from my toes to the top of my head. I had never had this feeling or experience in my life. Never! My logical mind had nothing more to say, and I shut it off. Finally I allowed myself to 'be'... How could I not?

Over the next couple of days we hung out and I just couldn't get enough of this man, but my darn logical mind is saying "run", "he is not the man for you" and my heart and soul were screaming to my head "shut up, who cares?" And again, fear was to take over and I ended things before they could go any further. Those feelings in my heart were scaring me and I just couldn't be open, or maybe just didn't know how. And so, against my heart and soul, it was over.

I was upset, beyond upset, and even mad at myself, but I knew that I obviously still had way too much healing and work to do on myself, in the relationship department. I continued to think of Mark a lot, how could I not? The experience with him was so incredible. Plus, I genuinely really liked him. I liked so many things about him, his kind, gentle nature and even the fact that he is quite charismatic. He is one of those guys who can say exactly the right thing, and, even if you know he is just trying to charm you, you don't seem to care because it feels nice anyways.

It's funny how we want something, in my case a relationship, and when it shows up, we run from it, even when our heart is screaming "NO, don't run." This is when we know we have a huge block and a lot of emotional healing to do,

Chapter 11
Breaking the Armour

This connection with Mark was not over, as Mark and I were to come back into each other's lives a few more times. The next time he was the one to reject me, which was very hard to take and the times after that I think that we just didn't know what to do about each other and worse yet, was that he would act interested in me, tell me he wanted a relationship, but then all of a sudden, he would push me away. Each time I did see him my heart would do the usual, and my soul yearned for him. I was getting so confused by all of this, and this time I begged for my Guidance to show me what the heck this was all about. It still took me a while to ask, as my ego mind forgets. I get so wrapped up in the chaos that it takes a bit to remember to ask for help.

My Guidance showed me that Mark was in my life to show me that I was disrespecting myself. "Disrespecting myself?" How? I thought I was doing better. All of that time I'd spent working on me and still I was disrespecting myself?

I was shown that all the times I was stressing over Devin's headaches, it was taking a toll on me and I was not being so gentle to myself. I was feeling like a failure as a mother and as a healer. I was getting mad and quite down, and I was starting to let my frustration get to me. You see, all those times when I was with Mark, my logical mind was fighting my heart and soul and would tell me to run. My logical mind knew, because I was told about some of Mark's past, by a few people that we mutually knew, about his past with women and how he was disrespectful towards them. I had a few people tell me that he was a player and to me a player was someone who does not respect. So, my own disrespect, out of stress and frustration, to myself came back as disrespect this time from Mark. But why did my heart feel the way it did, if he may have been a player? I believe that I would not have fully gotten the message if not for the intense feelings for Mark. If it was someone who I did not feel anything for, then I would not have cared enough and would not have had the experience of learning this important lesson. Plus, my heart and soul knew that Mark would show up again, with another lesson, and this time, to show me just how much I had been closing off my heart.

Now we come to the morning when I received a text from Mark, after I had asked the Universe for my next teacher. I was a bit surprised that the Universe brought Mark as my next teacher. I thought I would not hear from him again, but clearly I was very wrong, we texted the usual "How have you been?" "What's new?" Within a few days, he invited me to go visit him in the small town where he was living. Just before Mark's invite, I kept sensing that I was going to be going to the mountains and it was going to be life changing. I thought I was going on a spiritual trip or retreat in British Columbia or Jasper, Alberta, but the mountains that my intuition was referring to, were to be where Mark was living. The town he lived in was surrounded by beautiful mountains. I knew from my intuition and how intense it was, that I had to go, as it did say that it was to be life changing. That sounded wonderful! I kept asking my Guidance for more information, "Why am I going?" "Is it to finally be in a relationship with Mark?" The answer was, "No", just have patience, go unwind, observe and just be." I then asked if I would be moving to this town or somewhere close by. This time, all I heard was that I would find out the reason in due time, and to just enjoy being there. I have learned that sometimes we are to not know the answers and to just trust! I now know it to be because if we always know the answer to what is, then we can't truly enjoy the experience, to know ahead of time takes away the fun of unraveling the puzzle. So, because I trust my own Guidance and because I did enjoy being with Mark, I went. I went to see what is to be my life changing weekend.

Mark picked me up from the airport. I was feeling exited and that same electric feeling was to come over me. The drive to his house was to take a little over an hour and it was scenic. The mountains were so beautiful, the energy they emitted was so calming, and one can't help but be in awe of nature's creations. Mark would point out each mountain and its name, which ones he had hiked up, and even pointed to one called Heart mountain. "One can climb this mountain and claim that they will never get their heart broken again." Hearing Mark say this and the way he said it, alerted something in me. I should have known this was to be a clue on my journey, as I believe that when someone says something that makes you pay attention, upsets you or makes you really think, then there is a message, a hidden message for you to listen to, as it is always something you need to know about yourself. But, I think the view was so breathtaking that I just put it in the back of my mind and forgot about it until much later…

Now at Mark's house, I was starting to feel a bit uneasy, as I was sensing a bit of coldness from him. I could not read him and, for the next couple of days, I think my intuition was taken away from me. This does happen a lot when I am to just be in the moment and not know all of the answers. We were catching up on our life events since we last saw each other and I was still sensing that he may be holding me at arm's length. He seemed so distant and I was wondering if this had been a mistake, maybe I should not be there. And that electric feeling had diminished. I was confused, but I also knew that this was going to be another big lesson; "life changing." I would not have been originally guided otherwise.

The next day Mark had to work for a while, so I went shopping, had a massage, something that I don't do often enough for myself and then went for a steam. Later we had a wonderful supper. The restaurant had an amazing view of the mountains and our conversation was enjoyable, as it always was but I was still not getting that electric feeling. My heart and soul were just not doing what I was used to them doing around him. This was actually making me sad, because it was such a wonderful feeling before. We went back to his house and had a few glasses of wine. This was a bit unusual for me because I don't drink very often, but I decided to have a few glasses, maybe because I was feeling uneasy at Mark's distance or maybe because I just needed it. We both had a bit too much and we ended up making love. Well, honestly, it was more just sex this time, as I didn't feel the electricity and no connection at all and I still felt his coldness towards me. I was beyond confused and started wondering what this is all about. How can this be life changing when I am feeling this way? Things didn't feel awkward, just weird. I am not sure if, at the time, Mark was even aware of my feelings, and I was not ready to share them with him just yet.

The next day, we went for a walk to the river. It was a beautiful afternoon, the sun was out, I felt so peaceful, and we took a break and sat for a while. The sun in my face felt so good and the mountains around us were breathtaking. This was to become my new favorite place where my mind will go to while I sit silently during those times when I feel stress coming on or I just need to close my eyes and focus on something good, something beautiful, my new blissful place. In this spot, at the edge of the river, I felt like I was in the most loving, soft and gentle energy. It was amazing! I closed my eyes, laid back and asked that whatever this is all about that it be shown to me soon. I had trust in the Divine plan ahead of me and even thanked the Universe for setting it all up. If anything the break from work was all worth it, even if this was to be the only thing I was to take away from my weekend here.

The next day was my last and Mark drove me around the town and we got to see the sights. I left for home, with thoughts of the weekend swirling around my mind. But, I wondered why I did not have the same feeling as before when I was around Mark. I still really liked him and wanted a relationship with him, but maybe our time was to be done and whatever lesson, I was to learn was over.

But not just yet; Mark and I continued to text daily back and forth, nothing too important, just the odd "Good morning" and "How was your day?" I am still wondering, what was so life changing about this experience. About two days after I was home, I kept getting messages from my intuition to open up my heart to Mark. Open to Mark? But how, when I didn't feel the same intense electric feelings? How, with Marks coldness towards me? How, when all I was getting was a good morning text? I again heard "Just open and let your heart love him." It was not like we are in a relationship, so I don't think so! I was really starting to let my hurt ego ignore my intuition and decided to just give it a bit longer to integrate the message.

I allowed the message to sink in. I realized I needed to do what my intuition was asking, so I would allow it and observe what was happening or going to happen. That night at home, in a mindful meditation, I sat and pictured opening up my heart to Mark. I pictured him, his green eyes that light up when he smiles, his heart, and I thought about all the times I felt that electrifying feeling, that excitement from my soul. I imagined loving him, falling in love with him, and, honestly, it was quite easy and it felt genuine on some level, because I did have some feelings for him. I was really allowing myself to feel it with my whole being, every single bit of me. The energy in me started to rise and feel intense, and that is when it all happened, I felt my heart, I felt the armour around my heart break open, my heart, that was previously closed off from all of the past painful experiences, my heart that I vowed to never open again. I felt the armour was being removed and it was truly an amazing experience.

I just sat there and cried. I cried for how much I was shut off and I cried for how much damage I had done to myself by shutting off my beautiful heart, my heart that I thought was the best part of me. I had shut off the best part of me, as most of us do to prevent ourselves from getting hurt again.

I then realized that Joe, the man from my previous relationship, was just trying to love me. He was starting to fall in love with me and I knew and felt it, but as soon as he started to express it, my fear kicked in, as it always did around relationships. I ran. I shut him out. I didn't know how to receive his love. A heart that is built up with armour can't receive; the mind, out of fear, won't let it. I meditated a lot on all these thoughts and feelings, and I finally felt the toxic energy leave my body, the toxic energy that was blocking up my heart. And then the most elated feeling came rushing in. This was also when I was shown that this was the whole reason that my son, Devin, was getting headaches, he was my mirror. I froze. Oh My God!! My son was getting headaches because his chest was damaged from his fall, the fall that actually happened around the same time I vowed to never open my heart again and from me thinking that life had absolutely no joy. This was all because of me and my blocked heart. Talk about the worst feeling as a mother, but who knew? We finally figured out, after five years, why he was getting those horrible headaches. My Guidance told me to be gentle with myself and not to feel any guilt over this, but that's kind of hard to do, as a mother. I also knew that more guilt would just create something else negative. Instead of feeling guilty, I forgave myself, and allowed myself to be fine with it all. Then, I sent love and gratitude to Mark, for being the one to show up in my life at the perfect time, and for my son, Devin, for being my greatest teacher. To our relief, Devin's headaches just disappeared; all of a sudden, they were gone!

I will admit that a bit of doubt crept into my mind. It did sound a bit unreal that this was all because of me and my blocked heart, but I would be shown that it indeed was. Up to this point, Mark and I were still texting each other, usually just short messages. I could still feel his rejection of me, still holding me at arm's length, almost holding me on the back burner. It felt like he wasn't sure about me anymore. I am not saying this is what he was intentionally doing, but it is what I felt. And because I let my negative ego voice take over, and with the feeling of being rejected and upset, guess what I did? I closed my heart down again; I could feel myself shut off. I felt the energy shut off in my heart chakra, and almost immediately, Devin complained of a bad headache. This was definite proof that his headaches were from me closing off, so I sat down, meditated on opening up again and, within minutes, Devin's headache was gone.

Chapter 12
Our Souls can be very Deeply Connected.

So, Why Mark? Why did Mark show up and open this part of me, when no one else could? Why this man, who was showing up in my life as my reflection of disrespect, but who could also make my heart and soul vibrate with excitement? Mark's role was to be my teacher for these lessons, I just could not understand it at the time of our encounters. My Guidance tells me that Mark and I have shared many past lives together and that we are very connected on a soul level. Mark showed up and was perfect in this life time. My soul already knew him and recognized him on a soul level, and I needed him and his energy to help me with the lessons. Hence the reason for the soul excitement I was always getting around him, and he holding me at arm's length, which was actually brilliant, in the sense that it took his rejecting of me for my ego to get upset and try to shut down again, to really figure out that I indeed needed to reopen my heart and why Devin was getting headaches. Mark's and my soul were to keep guiding us to each other. I am not exactly sure what Mark's experience was or what, if anything, he felt. What I do know is that this man is special to me, and even though we do not connect with each other anymore, he will always have a place in my now open heart, and I am thinking that he will for several more lifetimes to come.

Since this experience with Mark, I now allow my heart to stay open. I use this experience to make sure that I never shut it down again, as I now know, if I am feeling love, feeling elation and open to receiving love, the Universe will respond by giving me what else… more love, of course!!

Soul Mates and Soul Connections

Soul connections are different from soul mates and we would like to think that both are the ideal romantic and perfect partner, that they are someone to complete us, and in truth, both are someone who is in our life to help us grow and we are, in turn, to help them. They do, at times, bring us our biggest challenges, but then again that is why we choose them and are drawn to them. In both cases of soul connections and soul mates, we share many past lives together and actually decide what we want to learn from each other before we incarnate again. We agree to help each other and how we are to connect.

Soul mates are people we have shared past lives with and who show up to help us on our journey. We can have several in one life time and they can be anyone from your sister, parent, brother, best friend, long life lover or anyone who shares a big part of your life and remains on your journey with you.

Soul connections, or what some call Twin Flames, need each other to accomplish a certain goal or mission together, and come together to help in areas where you could not do it by yourself. This is usually a strong connection and your soul will almost yearn for this person, as it knows they are the ones to help you in the area where you need it the most. We have no control over timing, or circumstances. Your souls will draw to each other and it will feel intense and as soon as you learn what you need, the energy will eventually fade away.

I also believe that if you are in search of your soul mate, in the sense of a romantic partner, then you first, and foremost, have to do your inner work to heal. You have to find yourself. You cannot attract "the one" until you fully love, honor and respect yourself. No one is going to come and save you, but you. You must learn how to fill your own heart and then you can be ready for "the one" to arrive. I am glad that I gave myself the gift of staying single for a long time, as this gave me the opportunity to learn who I was, what I needed to see in myself, and it taught me how to love myself, not to rely on anyone but me. The time, by myself, allowed me to see that I don't want a saviour, or an unrealistic relationship of just passion and unrealistic expectations, but instead, that I would like a partner to enjoy being with, a partner to help each other grow, learn and love.

The best example that I can give you about how we choose our soul connections and soul mates is this: just before we decide to incarnate on earth, we acknowledge we are coming to learn and grow for our soul's expansion. Our soul wants to continue to grow, but how can it grow in the place where it comes from? Where it originates is a place of pure unconditional love, (some call it heaven) but I think of it as another realm, as I believe that heaven is more a state of mind... In this realm all our soul knows is love, and so, it is hard to grow more love when it has no comparison to the opposite of love. Our soul doesn't know darkness because it is always light. So, it knows that earth is the place to learn. As we are in this place or realm of heaven, we are planning a lot of what we want to learn and who we want in our life. I will use myself as the example. I wanted to learn more, and grow more, and Greg's soul chose to come help me. This help was not by showering me with admiration, but by helping me to see the mirror, by helping me to forgive, to understand and grow from the experience with him. He is one of my many soul mates and he brought me some great opportunities and spiritual gifts. I could not have learned so much about the mirror or myself, if it were not for him. So, sometimes our soul mates and soul connections are actually here more to challenge us than to adorn us. I am fortunate enough to still be on friendly terms with Greg, which to some may seem a bit strange as he was not always so kind to me, but I know that I cannot hold onto anger or resentfulness. Holding onto these will only create more in my life and I know that he really didn't mean to be so hurtful, it was just his own pain that was actually acting out. I am grateful, for our children's sake, that we can at least be civil to each other.

I have also learned how to just observe myself and I now realize that I can learn so much about myself through my feelings. This was hard to do, in the past, as I was too shut down and had my armour built up around me. Now, I allow myself to feel, or better yet, understand what the feelings are all about. If I am sad about a situation, instead of getting upset, I ask myself "why did I attract a situation to me to make me upset, and why would this even make me upset?" I try to be the observer of my feelings and my reactions to them, even the good feelings. I look, as deep as I can, to figure out why. When one of the men on the dating site was talking too much about his ex-wife, my immediate reaction was frustration. It really bothered me, so I observed the feeling and then asked myself, "Why do I feel this way?" "What should I observe in myself that this feeling is being triggered?" That is when I realized I needed to work on an old issue with my ex-partner that I hadn't healed yet. I used to get a lot of anxiety, which to me is the worst feeling, and now if any anxiety shows up, I know this to be something very important I need to look into. Why am I feeling anxiety at the moment? Or, is this my own anxiety or someone else's that I am sensing?

When we learn to observe and listen, life seems to become more exiting! Everything seems to look so different. We learn to understand the bad things that happen to us and make them into useful situations to bring us learning and growth. They help us to build tools for our future experiences, so really, they are not necessarily bad as they bring growth and all growth is great.

I sometimes think of it as a puzzle with each piece fitting perfectly with the next, every piece making up the whole picture. Nothing ever happens by coincidence, everything really does happen for a reason. Because you have created it, your genius soul and the Universe conspire together to bring it all to you.

Devin continues to be almost headache free. I wish I could say he never gets them, but he does get the occasional migraine which is different than the ones he had before. This is most likely because he has some inner work to do, if and when he is ready to work on them, for even a migraine is your body's way of telling you that you need to listen and pay attention.

I wake up each morning in awe of this amazing journey of life. I look forward to all of the things that I will attract to me and for many more wonderful experiences. I know there is so much more to learn on this spiritual path, much more insight and knowledge that I have inside of me to teach others, but, for now, I sit and bask in all the glory. I am amazed and thankful at how far I have come, for knowing that there really is more to life than what we think, and for being able to help others on their healing and spiritual journey.

Before I felt guided to write my story, I was guided to take a step away from doing healing sessions, but at the same time, I wanted to continue to help others on their healing journey. Many people ask me what steps they can take, what is it they can do to heal themselves. I also wanted to share the spiritual side of my life, which is real for all, not just me. I wasn't necessarily given more gifts than anyone else, I just learned how to listen and connect or, better yet, reconnect with the spiritual realm and most important my Higher Self and Guidance. We are all connected and each one of us has our own Guidance and guides accompanying us, however we just can't hear or make sense of it all when we are in constant chaos in our mind or don't even know that they exist. If we don't give ourselves the time to quiet our mind and listen, then how are our Guides, or our Higher Self, going to reach us? And most importantly for parents, I wanted to show you just how much, your children are teaching you that you, too, need to heal. They are so connected to you, on every level, that if they are acting up, getting into trouble, or ill, then maybe it's time to look within yourself. As I mentioned earlier, they, too, have their own lessons to learn from the experiences with and without you, and this is why they chose you. I am thankful that my boys chose me, to both teach me and learn from me.

I also wanted to find a way to help anyone who has been physically and sexually abused. I, for so many years, diminished the events and acted like they did not matter and this was partly because I didn't think that I mattered. I would think, "Well, maybe I should have known better", or "Maybe I should not have been in the places I was, to have it happen." I even blamed myself for being physically abused and thought, for sure, that I must have done something wrong. Anything physically abusive is wrong... and anything sexual, that does not have your consent is a personal violation and it does not matter where you are, who you are with or what you are doing... it is wrong! Please get help to clear this energy from your being, so you, too, can heal and grow.

I wanted to reach out to anyone who has been through thoughts of suicide or the ones who also attempted it, in hopes their pain would be recognized or end. This issue has been ignored for too long and is still a taboo topic to talk about. There are women, men, teens and even young children, who are in such pain and turmoil that they feel alone, not heard, and have no idea how to deal with it all and so ending their life seems like the only way out of their pain. Sometimes we don't even know why we are so upset, as many people have buried their pain so deep and their armour is so big that they don't even know there are reasons for their pain. If this is you, then please find someone to talk to... a doctor, friend, therapist, or someone who does alternative healing therapy. If you are concerned about your child, then please talk to them and find out what is going on. It may not seem a big concern to you, but to them it can be too big of a problem to deal with on their own.

Many people turn to alcohol, drugs, sex and many other forms of addictions, even self abuse, in order to not feel or deal with their issues. They put all of their attention on something else in order to numb their inner pain. Why do you think so many people are addicts today? This is because no one knows how to deal with their stuff; this shows us there are so many people hurting. I am fortunate to have not turned to any substance, but I did find myself working way too much. This was not so much to not heal, but I used work as an excuse that I wasn't able to date. Even at the time, I knew, on some level, that I was not ready to see my issues with men. My beliefs around men became tarnished and, because of my experiences with them, I believed they were mean, selfish, emotionally unavailable, and only wanting a sexual relationship. I did hear often from a certain family member that "men will only want you for one thing, that's all they think about." Actually, I heard this a lot, and so it was to become part of my own beliefs. This is how someone else's beliefs can become your own. Even though this was their own truth, on their level, they really had no idea how much it was to influence me and my life. I now know that not only did I heal these issues, but that there are a lot of wonderful men in this world who are loyal, kind, emotionally available, sensitive, and nurturing and who know how to treat a lady with respect. This is now my belief, but again it took a long time to heal and treating myself with respect in order for me to understand this, heal it.

So, please be aware of what you are saying around your children, grandchildren or any children who are around you, even if it is something you believe to be true. Children listen on many levels and will believe everything that you say. Listen to your own beliefs and ask yourself why you believe them to be true. Change your words and I promise you that it will not only change yourself, but those around you, especially your children.

The Reflection

I look at you and see my friend, who's
sorrows and pain I pray to end.
You're someone I see as a shining light, which
brightens up the darkness of night.
Your kindness and love for others you share, to
show them how much you truly care.
The beauty that shines out from your soul, is
the one thing I wish for all to know.
I see your heart so full of love and grace, and
your words of wisdom I fully embrace.
I see in you so much good, even if at times you feel misunderstood.
You, to me, are the Divine perfection, and this is
when I was shown, you are my reflection.
I now see... I see that you are me.

Paige Orion

Chapter 13
What it is all about

The best way for me to describe everything in the spiritual sense, in my own way of understanding, is this, before we incarnate on this earth plane, we choose which people are to play important roles in our life, and who our parents and siblings are to be. I know some of you are shaking your heads and saying, "I don't think so, because I wouldn't pick the parents or siblings I have." Well, we actually do. We pick them because we, at that time being a soul, know that they are to be our teachers, and to show us what we want to grow in ourselves. Why? Again, when we are in the" realm" of heaven, we only know love. We don't have a contrast of what is not love and, believe it or not, we want to continue to expand in love. How can we expand love if all we know in this realm is love? We decide to come to earth, where we go through all of the dark periods, the pain and trauma, so that we can heal and grow our consciousness. We want to continue to create more love.

We also want to keep coming back, to either learn from the lessons we did not grow from in our past lives, or to continue to help each other, even the earth to grow consciously. It is hard for some people to believe that we have past lives, and I understand how it can seem so unreal but, from what I have been shown and told from my Guidance, past lives are all a part of our souls having human experiences. Isn't it nice to know that we can come back and have other experiences with our loved ones? I used to say, "Why on earth would I ever want to come back here?" "Here is hell!"(I believe hell, too, is a state of mind) I wanted to be done with this life and never have to come back. Obviously, it seemed like it was hell to me, as I was actually creating it to be so. I now love life and look at it differently. I look at it with amazement and awe. I am now living, or at least starting to live life, as we all should be, with excitement and joy. And, yes, I want the experience of coming back again and again, but, for now, I want to enjoy the rest of this life.

My Guidance tells me that these deep parts of my journey from my past are complete. This is not to say that other things won't come up or that I can't create something new to heal from, if I ever slip into old patterns. I am human, after all, or, better said, a soul having a human experience. If, for some reason, I do slip, then I will now have the knowledge and understanding that there is a reason, as well as the knowledge that I am creating each and every one of them. So, I think I will change my subject to love, happiness and joy. It seems so much easier now that I get it. This still seems a bit out of reach some days, but now I know to just 'be' and, most importantly, to be gentle with myself during these times. If I survived everything else, then, this small incident can be changed in a heartbeat.

The other thing I want to share is that we are constantly guided, by our Higher Selves which, are our souls, and by our Spirit Guides, Angels and everything that is connected to our souls. As I mentioned previously, we are all an aspect of God. Our souls are God and all is connected to the Universe, each other, animals, plants, everything. Our soul wants what is best for us, and is trying to help us on this journey of life. We receive signs that correspond with every thought and feeling that we have, and it is our job to pay attention.

The Universe is always speaking to us… sending us signs, messages, and synchronistic events. It, with your Higher Self, even sends us the right people to show up at the right time, to show, or tell you exactly what you need to hear, or to reflect back to you what you need, whether it be to learn or to show you that you are on the right track.

It will always send us the mirror that we need to see. I am happy to say that, now, my mirrors usually show up to reflect the growth in myself, the love I have, the wonderful opportunities, and all of the positive thoughts and feelings that I think and feel, most importantly about myself. If the mirror, shows up as negative, as they still do at times, then I look at where I need to change. I look for both the feelings in myself and the Universal signs to show me what I need to get back on track, or the signs that I may need when I am about to make an important decision.

Butterflies

For some reason, I have always known about these signs. I am not sure how old I was when I figured it out, or if it was just a knowing, within myself, but I remember asking for signs when I was quite young. I wasn't as aware back then and had no idea that everything is a sign. I just asked for small signs at certain times in my life. One particular sign would show up as butterflies. I always had a passion for these creatures and when I needed a positive sign, they would magically show up. I knew that somehow they were placed in the right spot when I needed them. Eventually, I paid attention and I would notice other things as signs, some were positive and others were negative. Not only would they show up when asked, but they showed up even if I was just thinking of something negative or positive. They showed up to tell me that I was, or was not, in alignment with what my soul wanted for me.

I tell my clients to pay attention, as all signs that you see are meant for you. What I get as something positive may be something else for you. If you notice something showing up often, like a certain animal, song on the radio, numbers, people, or you keep seeing or hearing something, then pay attention to what is going on at that moment. Were you just angry, mad, happy or thinking something positive? Then this is a clue as to what that sign will always mean for you and so the next time that you see or hear it, you will make the connection.

I use my signs every day, all day. In fact, they just show up and one of the best times my signs came in handy was when I bought my salon. I was scared and I imagine for anyone, buying a business is scary. I remember wanting to buy it, but worried about not being able to support myself (remember that story) as my ex-partner, Greg, had no intentions of helping me in any way. The month was November, almost winter, so quite chilly out. I was driving to the salon to see it for the first time, and on my way, I asked my Guides to show me a butterfly, "actually, show me several." I knew it was a tall order, but, I also knew if it was for me to buy then I would get my sign. Well, I didn't see any butterflies on my way there, but when I walked into the salon. There were several ceramic butterflies around the salon, and on the mirror, there were three glass winged butterflies, my absolute favorite. I knew the shop was to be mine and trusted that it would all work out. And has it ever! I am grateful for that space and for each and every client who comes in, for they are all gifts who bring me a message or reflection each and every day.

I try to pay attention to each client's stories, or anything they have to say to me, as I not only enjoy hearing them, but I also know that there is a message for me, as well. One lady talked about her grandson and told me a cute story about how he "likes to keep his words in." This was how he was telling her when he didn't want her to question him on something that he had just done. The way she said it made me aware that I, also, hold my words in at times, because I still find it a bit hard to fully speak my truth. Not that I lie, but sometimes it is easier to just keep my words in, because I still feel scared of confrontation or hurting someone's feelings. This does no one any good, but it showed up in a client, talking about her grandson, for me to learn.

These signs have been guiding me, through every part of my life. They show up to tell me everything from what vitamins are good or not good for me; what negative or positive thoughts I am thinking or are unaware of; if I should turn right or left; and even helped guide me on my dating experiences. Now, that I am much more aware of them, and they are also a part of my Guidance system, especially when I am in a bit of a chaotic state and cannot listen to my Guidance, it sends me physical signs to help me out.

So, how does one know what their signs are, and isn't that a lot of work? Well, it seems like a lot of work, but it's really not. It can be a lot of fun. I tell my clients to just pay attention. If something keeps showing up on your path, then go to what you were just thinking, saying or doing. If you keep seeing, a crow, then pay attention to what you are thinking at that time. For me, I noticed that crows appear to show me that I am on the right path, more so if they fly across my path. A magpie, on the other hand, will always show up to tell me that I am on the wrong path or that what I am about to do should not happen. You can also meditate and ask your Higher Self or Guidance to show you what may be your positive and negative signs.

I now have many signs that my Guidance shows me and these signs never fail me when they show up. Even numbers on a licence plate, or on a clock, are signs. Along with butterflies, I remember always seeing the number forty-four. It was starting to drive me crazy when I realized they were showing me that I was in the right direction and in alignment with my soul. My signs are always accurate. This concept also helps us to get out of our monkey brain where our thoughts, are all over the place, and we are thinking so many different things in a minute that we don't even know how to live in the moment. Paying attention to your outer world helps you figure out your inner world, and helps you to live more in the here and now and not in the past or future.

The other reason I believe we receive signs is because we don't always know what is best for us. I once read that you should respond only by how you feel. I understand feelings help us to figure out why we draw things to us, but one should not rely only on their feelings. One can feel good eating a full bag of candy, but it is obviously not good for us, or one can feel good by drinking a bottle of wine, but, as most of us know it's really not in our best interest. One may feel good about a lot of things that really are not good for us. How about when we are angry at someone and we want revenge. Sure the satisfaction of revenge would feel good, but in the long run we are just hurting ourselves. I have had times that I did not feel good about a situation or person, but my soul wanted me to be in that situation for a lesson I needed to heal and so I received positive signs to guide me and show me to continue on until I received the lesson. I have also been in situations that were fun and made me happy, but, would get a lot of negative signs to tell me that this was not a healthy situation, even if it felt good. So, yes, feelings are great, but I don't believe that they are always to guide us.

Daisies

Another sign, that would pop up, around my whole experience with Mark was Daisies. "Why, daisies?" I asked my Guidance. I was to be patient for the answer. For some reason, I would see daisies in my mind's eye the second time I was to connect with Mark. It seemed to be, that every time I saw a picture of a daisy, either on the internet, in a magazine, on someone's shirt or actual daisies, I would soon hear from him. Mark, of course, had no idea, as how do you tell a man that daisies appear around him as one of my signs? Well, one night when I was at Mark's house, we talking about ourselves as young children and he went into another room and came out with a large picture. He turned it around for me to see and here he was around the age of five, mountains behind him and he was sitting in a field of daisies! I think I remember laughing out loud, as that was clearly why I was seeing daisies around him. I had no choice but to share my daisy signs with him. I believe this particular sign was given to show me that I was on the right path with Mark. So, now when I see daisies, I can't help but think, not only of Mark and my experience with him, but to think of them as a reminder to be sure I am staying open. I am also, just now, seeing the connection to the mountains. Not only were they a part of his picture, but they were to be a part of my connection with going to see him in the mountains.

Mirror, Mirror

As, I have mentioned throughout my story, people show up to mirror us. Well, it's not just family members, it can be anyone. Each client who comes into my salon will be a mirror for me. It might be one word they say, or something that they are going through that is reflecting something that I need to look at in myself or it may be a message of encouragement that I just need to hear at that moment. Sometimes it may be something they say that makes me wonder "Why did they just say that?" If you can't figure out right away what it means, keep a mental note, as it will be made known eventually.

It seems the people who make us the angriest, or the people we just don't seem to like, always have one of the biggest reflections for us to look at. Your soul actually attracted them to you, to teach you this lesson, and the reason they upset you so much is because your soul is trying to get your attention. Once you understand this and get the lesson, the person will either never cross your path again or the next time they do, you just won't seem to care. They may even become your new friend.

As I have so many experiences in my life, I will share the one of the egotistical young man. As I mentioned before, my salon has helped me grow and I have learned so much while being there. Again, I had a problem with people parking in my three stalls that were for my clients. (This too was always to reflect something that I was going through.) This young man parked in my spot and I politely asked him to move and he, more or less, told me off and stayed in that spot. I was mad! I was about to call a tow truck, but then he did end up leaving. This young man had just moved into the building where my salon is located and this game continued for a week or so. I was starting to get quite upset when I heard myself calling him, a little egotistical brat. Yep, I got it! I had to look at where my own ego was acting up, and acting like a little brat.

We are Vibrational Beings

As I spoke of earlier, we all have vibrational frequencies. In these frequencies, I see it as an aura around a person. This aura is with us since birth and holds all of your pain, worries, thoughts, feelings, beliefs, ideas, good or bad and the vibration of how you feel about yourself, life and others. It holds all of your energetic information and, if the energy of all of this is negative, it will also affect your chakras and eventually it's what affects our physical bodies as it manifests as illness or disease. We don't necessarily have to have the actual memory of such events to be in our aura, as we do forget a lot of our memories plus, sometimes, we don't think that something small can affect us, but the energy of the event will stay in the aura. When I am doing a healing session for a client, I am actually feeling and sensing what is in this vibrational, energetic aura and in their chakras. I have had clients come in confused as they keep drawing certain situations to them, but they can't figure out why, they have no memory of what to heal. This is when I can help, I see it in their aura, and help them to heal and clear it. There are many wonderful energy facilitators who do this kind of work, so if you feel that you have something that you just cannot heal in yourself, then please find someone to help.

So, when I was in my not-loving-myself state, and having all of the negative thoughts about myself, plus all of the un-healed energy of the sexual, physical and emotional abuse, I was adding all of this to my aura. The vibration of my aura was dense and slow moving; it was weak from me not having any boundaries and from allowing so many negative thoughts and feelings to consume me. My aura was actually weak and had many rips and tears in it.

These rips and tears were from all the attacks towards me from others and myself, and they were what allowed other's negative energy in. Their negative thoughts and feelings got into my aura and this is why I sensed and felt those thoughts and feelings, but thought they were my own. The rips and tears allowed what good energy I did have, to seep out. When we have bad boundaries, allowing others to treat us badly and allowing our own self to treat ourselves badly, we absorb all of this bad energy into our aura. We can also attract and absorb all of the fear, negativity or happy, positive frequencies of what is happening in our community, our Country, and even the world.

If we are watching a lot of news, listening to everyone talk about how bad the economy is or how much violence there is, and all the "bad" in our world, what we are actually doing is allowing all of that fear and chaos into our aura. This creates fear, and fear is a low vibrational frequency which will negatively affect us and lower our frequency. This is why I don't watch the news; I actually don't even watch T.V. unless it's a fun, uplifting program. I also try not to engage in gossip. Firstly, talking bad about someone else is not a nice thing to do, as it doesn't make one look better, it actually lowers your vibration. So, when I am around someone who wants to talk about what is on the news or what a horrible person so and so is, I quickly re-direct the conversation as I don't want to lower my vibrational frequency, and allow this negativity into my aura. But at the same time I have to ask myself, why did I attract someone to me who has this frequency of gossip or negativity? This is a chance for me to look at where I may still have some of this in myself. I ask myself, 'was I recently maybe gossiping' or 'was I allowing the negative ego voice in recently'?

This vibrational aura attracts people who have the same vibrational frequency to us, as like-attracts-like. So this, too, is what gets sent out and returned to us from the Universe.

The lady in my parking lot, who I talked of earlier and who was not nice to me, would have had some similar vibrational frequencies as myself.

If I was not in this lower frequency, then this incident would have never happened. If I was in a higher frequency, I would not have drawn her to me for this lesson as the frequency has to match. She either would not have parked there, or she would have been more polite to me, as we both would have been in a higher vibrational energetic frequency.

Think about the word 'hate'. Can you feel how dense and uneasy you feel just by saying it? It has such a low vibrational tone to it, as words also carry a frequency in them, and that is why we can feel so drained after talking negatively. Do you really want that feeling of negative vibration in you? Now think about the word 'love'. Say it and feel it. Can you feel the vibrational tone of it? Doesn't it feel better? It's the same with saying 'thank-you'. When I affirm thank-you, I am also raising my vibration. When I tell myself that I 'love' me, I am raising my vibrational frequency and that is also why I can now attract more loving people to myself. My loving frequency attracts the same.

Once we start to heal, change our beliefs, words and feelings into positive ones, then all of the density from the negative can leave our aura, and our vibrational frequency starts to become less dense, and moves at a faster rate. The rips and tears start to heal so that nothing negative can come in and all of our good and positive stays within our aura. We become healthier, not just emotionally but physically as well, because in a high vibrational state, only positive can thrive. Our chakras move and spin at a balanced rate and we become healthier, happier and more loving and this will attract that same energy frequency to us which will continue to help us become higher vibrational beings.

Everything has a vibrational frequency to it as everything is energy, even plants and animals. They too have a vibrational frequency, and just like our children, they too absorb our energy. Your plants and animals can mirror you as well. They absorb our energy and can become ill. If your pet is not well, chances are that you have something going on within yourself that needs to be addressed. Many times I've heard people talking about "what a coincidence" that their pet has something medically going on as they do. My dog, Sam, used to be very scared and full of anxiety, and this makes sense, as now I understand that he was picking up on me. He held that scared, anxious energy inside of him having absorbed it from me. Our pets can sense our energy very well, and can tell when we are upset; they look down, are sad and may even want to sit with us. When we are happy and loving, they feel this too, and will show it. They will mirror us.

This, too, is why animals can sense a kind person. They can feel the person's vibrational frequency and know that they will be safe, or the opposite, if they don't like someone, chances are they can feel and sense it emitting from them and they know that their vibrational frequency is not nice.

My brother-in-law, Ken, is an animal magnet. Animals just love him and are always drawn to him. Ken is a very gentle, loving person who loves animals and would do anything for anyone. His energy is very caring and animals sense this and go to him, as they know he's kind and safe.

My grandma had a houseplant that was so beautiful. It had the longest vines wrapping around her entire kitchen. At certain times of the year, it would blossom into the most beautiful flowers which filled the room with a particular sweet scent.

Grandma would transplant pieces of her plant, and give them to all of her family and friends, as everyone loved it and would ask about it.

One day sitting around her kitchen table with family, we were admiring the blossoms; I mentioned that my plant never blossoms. Grandma gave it to me many years prior, it seemed my plant was slow growing and never once blossomed. My aunt told me that it was because it didn't like the energy of my house. 'Really'? I thought. This was many years before I knew of energy and vibrational frequencies. My house at the time was the one I shared with Greg.

Shortly after I moved out, my plant finally blossomed. I lost count of how many flowers were on it and it still blossoms to this day. I guess back at the time, my plant really didn't like the negative energy. I also like to think that maybe it's a way for my grandma to say hi and that she is glad to see me so happy.

Let's all raise our vibrations! When we do, it's good for us and it also helps the vibrational frequency of everything around us. It goes out to the collective of everyone and will actually help change the vibrational frequency of our world. When we help ourselves, we also help everyone else.

Everything Happens for a Reason

Absolutely everything happens for a reason, because we draw it to us. Everything happens to show us where we are at. Instead of asking, "Why did this happen to me?" ask yourself "Why did I draw this situation or person to me and what does my soul want me to know from this experience?" If you ask, and give yourself the time and space to listen, you will always get the answer. We are not victims, we are creators. Things do not happen to us, things happen because of us. A lot of people, including myself, at one time want to be a victim and think that life and people are just mean to them. They may even crave the attention that they receive when they tell their stories of all of the bad things that have happened to them, which really is showing others how much turmoil is in their thinking. When you step out of being a victim, you find your true power, you grow in consciousness, and you learn to love life because now you can create the life you truly want.

Everything in our outer world is connected to what is going on in our inner world. Did your car overheat? Maybe you are working too hard. Are your taps constantly leaking? It is most likely a reflection of your inner emotions. Did your doorknob fall off? This may be a reflection that you need to get a handle on things. Is your foot hurting for no reason or you keep stubbing your toe? Chances are, you need to move forward in an area of your life and you are ignoring it.

I have a client who kept getting hurt. She, in only one week, cut her finger quite badly, banged up her knee, hit her head on a cupboard, fell down her stairs and bruised her tailbone. I showed her that these hurtful events were her creations of how she was talking to herself in a very hurtful way. I showed her that they were happening to her, because her inner hurtful words were manifesting into hurtful injuries, including her vehicle getting a big dent in the side while in a parking lot.

This may be a new concept to some, but it will never fail you if you start paying attention. There is always a connection. The Universe and your soul will bring a circumstance to you to show you what you need at the time. My Mom asked me, "How can this be?" "How can your car have anything to do with you?" Well, each and every thing is a reflection of you, everything! This is how amazing and powerful we are, as well as the Universe. I have seen it so many times in my life and know not to question it, but to trust in it.

While in one of the past relationships I was in, I started getting tendonitis in my arm. It took me a while to understand that forearm tendons are for the muscles in our hands that we use to grab with. It was a sign for me that this relationship was not good, and I needed to "let it go". As soon as we ended things, my arm started to get better.

One day I came home from work, in the middle of winter, and my door would not open. It was stuck, and I tried everything to open it. I ended up calling my brother-in-law to help. After he finally fixed the problem, I sat down and realized that it was a sign for me to not go ahead with a situation I was thinking about. I was planning to go to a Christmas party with a friend the next day, but I felt in my intuition that I should not go. But, because I wasn't doing anything anyways and I was getting tired of being bored, I thought I would go. After the incident with my door, I decided that I would not attend the party as this was a big enough incident to happen for me to understand. It turns out that everyone at the Christmas party got bad food poisoning from the supper. Had I gone, I would have been sick, too. I would have been out of work for a few days and this would have been the worst time of year, as a hairdresser, to be ill. Christmas season is our busiest time. To rearrange all my clients would have been impossible. I know that the Universe, our Guides and Higher Selves all work together to make everything and anything happen to help us, in one form or another.

Loving and Honoring Yourself

I have mentioned throughout my story, many times I created negative events because I wasn't loving and respecting myself. These were some big events that were created out of it all, but, it's not just the big negative thoughts and feelings that can create chaos in our lives.

Lack of love, and respect for yourself can be in many forms. Did you skip a meal today, because you want to lose weight? Or maybe you were so busy that you just didn't make the time to eat, to nourish your body. Did you go for another cup of coffee instead of a glass of water? Are you eating food that is not healthy, and not getting enough sleep. Staying at work longer than your body can handle, this too, is not respecting yourself, and will create chaos in your life. Did you get cut off in traffic recently, this to me is a sign of disrespect, and would be reflecting on you, disrespecting yourself someway.

Another form of not honoring yourself is saying "yes" to someone, when you really mean "no". Doing things out of obligation or from guilt, is really going against yourself, and how you really feel.

Something as little as saying, "gosh, was I ever stupid for saying that" or for "doing that" is going to create something negative. As I mentioned, our words, and feelings go out to the Universe and will come right back to us, in one form or another.

These are all things that are non-loving, and are disrespectful towards yourself. I worked a lot, as a single mother; I had a belief that I had to work hard and long hours in order to provide for my son, and myself. I was working long hours. I was putting my clients before myself, and worse yet, I was putting money before myself. I was showing myself that I wasn't worthy of having time for me.

Once I realized this and cut back my hours, I actually started making more money. I started honoring myself, and I put me first. How is that possible you may wonder, well again, when we put ourselves first, the Universe provides. It will reflect this in you. I remember one December; I was working long hours as December is my busiest time of the year and I didn't want to have a client not be able to get their hair done for Christmas. So, in my exhausting myself, my vehicle reflected me, and broke down. The fan, that cools the engine down quit working, and my vehicle overheated. I knew exactly what it meant; I was over working and needed to 'cool down'. So, the extra money that I did make that month, well, it went towards my vehicle being fixed.

When I quit working so hard, my outer world reflected this and I don't have the extra expenses of things breaking down, plus, things just seem to fall into place, because I now know that the Universe always supports me as I am supporting, loving, and respecting myself.

A client of mine was having issues with his hot water tank in his house. He went through 3 of them within 2 years. On top of this, his house dryer quit working, and then the heat from his furnace wouldn't kick in to heat up his house. It didn't take long to realize that, this was reflecting how much he disliked his job. He complained of how much he disliked his job, but was staying because the money was so good. His dislike was turning into anger, and he was getting 'hot tempered' at work, as well as bringing his temper home. He was putting money before himself, and staying at a job he disliked so immensely, was starting to create the chaos in his house.

So, putting money and a job before himself was disrespecting himself, and again, the extra money he was making was just going towards fixing his house.

When we take the time to honor, and respect ourselves, we always get the same in return. This was a hard belief for me to really believe, as I couldn't possibly figure out how my vehicle could be my reflection, but as I know now, everything is!

Take care of yourself. Have a hot bubble bath, take a nap, relax, as what needs to be done, can wait for a bit. Put yourself first. Love yourself. Don't let the little things like skipping a meal turn into a chaotic event to have to show this to you.

Let the Universe reflect in you the love, and respect, you have for yourself, I promise that it will show you in the most amazing ways.

My hope for everyone is to start healing, and free yourself from the armour, blocks, guards and masks that you put around yourself, especially to be free of the negative ego voice that seems to control so much of our negative thinking. Life really is meant to be a journey. Quit taking things so seriously and start living the life that your soul wants for you. Wake up every day and be thankful that you are alive, that you are breathing, and look for all of the gifts that you draw to yourself. You may not believe in any of these concepts, and if they don't feel true to you then by all means, find something that does fit for you. I believe that if I can come out of my pain and sorrow and learn to understand all of this, then so can you.

Gratitude and Forgiveness

If it all seems like too much and you are having struggles, one of the best things to do, in the beginning of your journey, is something that I still do each and every day, think and try to feel what you are grateful for and write it in a journal. I start and end each day saying thank you. In the morning I am grateful for my warm bed, having a safe night, my dog Sam, who greets me with a hug before I get up. I am grateful for the health and wellbeing of my family. I will even say thanks for the amazing day that is ahead of me. Throughout my day, I say thanks for my clients for showing up and trusting me to not only do their hair, but for feeling safe that they can tell me their stories. I am thankful for my healing clients, who feel safe and trust in my knowledge and healing abilities. I am thankful for my connection to God, my Higher Self, the Universe, my Guides, and the texts that I receive from friends, family and my sons. At night I reflect on my day and am thankful for each and every thing that happened, yes even the bad things as they too are a gift. I promise that by always being in a state of gratitude, you will always have reasons to be thankful and you will receive more to be thankful about. This truly creates miracles.

And one cannot fully heal if they cannot forgive. You first need to understand that you are not a victim of other people's doings. You have created it all. So, forgive the wrong doings, the wrong doers and most importantly yourself. I forgive my cousin, my parents, Greg, the egotistical brat, even the egotistical brat within myself, any friend who hurt me in the past, any and everyone, for they all showed up at the perfect time on account of myself. I also forgive myself. Sometimes it's hard and it may take me a bit to forgive, if I am still angry. I allow myself to feel it, so that I don't suppress anything and become blocked again, but then I release it. The anger may come up again, and again I allow it until it is gone for good. I just observe, learn and release it.

Anger and not forgiving is toxic. It leads to toxic and negative thoughts, and feelings which will only create illness in yourself. I don't hate the men who molested me. I forgive them. They would have no idea of my anger and would not care. My anger would not affect them, it would only affect me. It would keep me as a prisoner in my own mind, so why should I let these incidents ruin the rest of my life by hating them?

I believe we are all good and loving on a soul level. There are no evil people, just people who are blocked from their soul, from God. Let's forgive them and send them love, as they must be in a great deal of pain to feel the need to lash out at others. Everyone is just trying to live, find a morsel of happiness, and most of all to find self love. This does not mean you should be around them. If they are toxic and mean, due to their ego voice and pain, then stay clear of them. If you can find it in yourself, send them love, for that is not only what they need, but maybe what you need too.

To Love Unconditionally

So many things have been shown to me and another I have learned about loving myself is learning not to be a people pleaser. My first and foremost job is about loving myself and putting me first. This is very opposite from what we are taught, but in me trying to get everyone to like me and me always doing things for others, ended up leaving me depleted of my own energy. I wanted my ex-partner to love me only because I didn't love me, so in a way this is being selfish. I was actually doing a lot of good things for him and others out of personal gain. "If I do this for you, I hope you will like me for it." This becomes conditional. True love, or even just helping others, should have no conditions on it.

When we learn to love ourselves unconditionally and learn to fill ourselves up first, we will then have enough. We will then do things for others only if it aligns with our soul, and only if it is not out of need within ourselves. Then it becomes unconditional. Then and only then, it becomes unselfish.

I know many people want to volunteer or help others in need, just to put it on their resumes or to boast in front of others. They want to be sure that everyone else sees them as a "good person," mostly because they cannot see this within themselves. They actually do it out of selfishness, not fully out of their heart. They are not bad, they just don't understand that they are lacking their own needs and to, first and foremost, take care of themselves; otherwise it's the negative ego that gets fed.

I am all about helping one another because we are all connected. It really does feel good to help others, but be cautious that the negative ego isn't doing it out of feeling 'better than'. I used to see a homeless person on the streets and I would say, "Bless that poor soul." This actually was making me on some level, feel higher than them and feeding my negative ego. Now, if I see someone who is either homeless or does not have as much as myself, I say "Namaste." This to me, means, my soul sees the Divine God who lives in you, just as you see the Divine God who lives in me. This means that I see your soul wanting to have a human experience in this life situation and I will not judge it in anyway.

Affirmations

You can also use affirmations to help you heal or just to help you as a daily tool. An affirmation is a saying that you repeatedly say to yourself. Like the time I had to tell myself to be gentle with myself. I have said so many over the years and I know they work. The trick is that you have to believe it and feel it to be true.

Another example, if you are feeling unlovable, is to close your eyes and think of a time when you really did feel love from another. It may have only been one time with your grandmother, or one time in a past relationship. It does not matter who you are with or what you were doing; what matters the most is how it felt. As you sense the feeling, repeat to yourself, "I am lovable, I am worthy of love" or whatever saying feels true to you. Over time you will start to believe it and it becomes your new belief pattern and reality, and you will draw loving people and events to you, which will reflect your new belief.

Some of my favorite affirmations that have worked for me are-

- I love life and life loves me.
- All I see is love.
- The Universe supports me, I am safe and secure.
- I am grateful for my abundance.
- Money flows easily and freely to me.
- I now attract loving and loyal people to myself.
- I love my career, clients and I love the flexible hours I have.
- I feel peaceful each and every day.
- I am grateful for all of my friends, family and people who truly accept me in my life.
- I am open to the higher wisdom within myself.
- I am joyful, loving, happy and elated.
- I am grateful for my health.
- Harmony, beauty and joy now surround me.
- I now create all good things for myself
- I now attract everything that aligns with my Higher Self.
- Who I am makes a difference.
- The Universe conspires with my Higher Self.

Find what feels true to you. You may want to write them on post-it notes and place them around your house, office or car to remind yourself to say them. Then do it as these little sayings are beyond powerful.

I have a ribbon that a wonderful client gave me which reads, "Who I am makes a difference." I placed it in the back of my salon, where I eat and meditate in-between clients, and it is right there for me to see and read. I make a point of reading it with a smile on my face and gratitude in my heart for her sharing it with me, as well as the feeling of, yes, who I am really does make a difference.

Anything affirming will benefit you. Remember when I was affirming thanks for my ex-partner in supporting our sons, or the time I affirmed thanks for Devin's healing? Not only was I being thankful, but I was affirming as if it had already taken place and so it became real, and then the Universe delivered it to me.

Besides going to that amazing place in my mind, the one by the river, in the mountains, where I was with Mark, the best thing for me to do, to feel good, is to think about the things that make me smile. I have so many now, but my favorite is thinking of the times when my boys Justin and Devin hug me and say that they love me. I go to these memories to lift my spirits if I need a little support or encouragement in my day. When I started doing my affirmations, it was a bit hard as some of them just didn't feel true. I couldn't bring in a feeling to make the affirmation real to me, so instead I would think of these times with my boys while I was affirming and what a difference it made. It all felt real as it brought a good feeling to it.

Please give yourself time, lots of time, to heal as it does not happen overnight. Be gentle with yourself and know that you are always exactly where you need to be. I am still learning this one. I think I am almost there, but I still need to work on it at times.

Let go of trying too hard and trying to control it all. Just allow the process to happen, listen to that inner voice that gut feeling, and, by all means, do not diminish anything that seems like a vision. They are real, and are from your Higher Self and your Guides.

Become the observer. Observe your emotional pain, and frustrations, the constant stream of negative thoughts and emotions that run through your mind and the sad stories that keep feeding your pain. Choose not to identify yourself with them for the stories are not you, they are made up by the negative ego voice, keeping you trapped. See yourself almost on the outside as the one who's observing all the emotional pain and the discomfort, but do not make the pain a part of who you are. Don't make it your endless life story. Don't claim and hold onto it tightly as your own, otherwise, you will continue to create more of the same, and then the negative ego voice wins.

I am grateful for each and every person and experience that I have had in my life. Each moment, good and bad, has molded and shaped me into the person who I am now, and I honestly can say the person I am now is wonderful. I am finally at peace, and I love and respect myself. I know I may have a few bumps along the rest of my journey, but they, too, will mold me into my future me. Life is great!

I am grateful for all of my spiritual and non spiritual teachers, who help me put the pieces of the puzzle together when I was a tad confused. I even had a spiritual teacher who showed me how not to teach, as his way was a little too harsh for me. I am thankful to all my teachers, the ones who show up exactly on time when I need them. I am grateful! There is a saying that I have come to learn as truth, which is, "When the student is ready, the teacher will appear, and when the teacher is ready, the student will appear." For we are all teachers and students learning from one another.

I want to also mention that I have had many good things happen to me over the years, that I have attracted to myself. They were not all bad, but my focus wants to be on showing you how to heal the bad, the painful moments, as they seem to be what we hold onto the most. I want to show you that you're creating them and how to change your creations into joy, happiness, peace and, above all, love.

May you find peace, joy and love, first within yourself, as then, and only then, the wonderful, amazing, loving Universe will send more your way.

Namaste.

! Close My Eyes and Take a Breath

I close my eyes and take a breath, as something inside me stirs and I cannot rest.

My soul awakens as I cry and whispers softly "please continue to try."

There is love, please don't give up hope, as deep
within you shall find ways to cope.

Peace is yours if you heal inside, with your
guides and angels close by your side.

When your faith is lost or weak, remember it
is your own love that you truly seek.

There are signs to help you on your way; the
Universe helps you each and every day.

For answers, you make look up to the sky and
there you will find your very own butterfly.

Many lessons I have learned, and it was self-
kindness and love that my soul did yearn.

When your heart is open wide, the love will
flow and heal you deep inside.

Through your tears, your healing shall start, but it
may take you to open up your broken heart.

I am glad I listened to that gentle voice for
now my soul can relax and rejoice.

I close my eyes and take a breath.

Paige Orion

Chapter 14
Where does one begin?

I have listed the things here to help you start on
your journey. Do what feels right and you can
do them in order of what works for you.

Journaling: Buy yourself a nice journal if you want to. I used normal
scribblers as, I have to admit I needed the room. I had a lot to write
about.

Writing letters: to anyone you feel the need to.

List's and your mirrors: Single out one person who is upsetting you
at the moment and list all the things they are doing or saying that
are bothering you. After you have written them, read them and
look for the mirror. Look at what they may be saying and doing
to you that, on some level, you may be doing to yourself. Are they
rude? Maybe you have been rude towards yourself. Are they always
late and disrespectful of your time? Maybe you are disrespectful
towards yourself or others somewhere and this needs to come to your
attention. Their actions may even reflect the opposite, meaning that
if it bothers you that they are too loud, maybe this is a sign that you
are to quiet and need to speak up.

<u>In touch with your feelings</u>: Start with how you are feeling right now… sad, mad, angry, happy? Write about these feelings and why you think you are feeling them. Let the words flow. It may seem a bit odd at first, as it was for me. I remember not knowing what to write, but once I started it became easy.

<u>Say Thank you</u>: I like to take to say thanks for this clarity when I am in any situation. I believe it helps bring understanding to a new experience, as this is not only true, but can bring more things to be grateful for… If we are not grateful for what we already have then how can we be open to receive more?

<u>Meditating</u>: I would recommend just trying it. I know we all struggle finding time for ourselves, but I would strongly suggest you make time. Again, don't get discouraged. Start with just sitting quietly for a few minutes, close your eyes, and concentrate on your breathing. Take long, deep breaths and, in time, you will learn how to clear your mind and listen to your Guidance more clearly.

<u>Try to reconnect with your younger-self</u>: Find a picture of you at a young age and or close your eyes and imagine yourself as a little girl /boy and talk to her/ him. Ask her/ him what you can do to help them. Imagine your adult-self hugging your younger-self and telling your younger-self that you are sorry that they are hurting, sorry that they had to go through anything that upset them. Tell her/him that you are here for them now and that you love them. This may seem a bit hard at first, but this exercise is a profound healing technique.

<u>Affirmations</u>: Say them as many times as you need to. Say them when you're tempted to say something negative. Say them every time you think of it, you will be amazed at how they work miracles.

<u>Reading</u>: Find as many self-help books as you can and then do the inner work. Don't just read about what to do. Follow the advice and put it into a daily practise.

<u>Surround yourself with positive</u>: Find anything positive to make your journey more enjoyable. Find a spiritual teacher who can give you tools that work for you. Searching for people, who are on the same journey as you, will attract them to you and you can share your experiences together.

<u>Find the time</u>: You, above everyone else, need your own time. By doing this you will show the Universe that you matter, that you are important to you and then you will receive more positive back from the Universe.

Good luck and never forget… who you are
matters and makes a difference.

I bless you with grace, for the brilliant soul that you are. May abundance fill your life and may you find peace, joy and happiness within every moment of your day. Be thankful for all of your blessings so that the Universe may shower you with more.

Paige Orion

About the Author

Paige is a mother, hairstylist, intuitive healer, and a spiritual teacher. She's learned how to heal herself from past traumas and events using her intuition and other helpful tools she gained along the way. She found her own self-empowerment and now shares and helps others on their healing journey.

E mail- paigeorion@outlook.com
Web page- www.paigeorion.net

Printed in the United States
By Bookmasters